HOW TO KEEP GOD ALIVE FROM 9 TO 5

John V. Chervokas

BERKLEY BOOKS, NEW YORK

This Berkley book contains the complete
text of the original hardcover edition.
It has been completely reset in a typeface
designed for easy reading and was printed
from new film.

HOW TO KEEP GOD ALIVE FROM 9 TO 5

A Berkley Book, published by arrangement with
Doubleday and Co., Inc.

PRINTING HISTORY
Doubleday and Company edition/January 1986
Berkley edition/June 1987

ISBN: 0-425-09893-1

A BERKLEY BOOK® TM 757,375
Berkley Books are published by The Berkley Publishing Group,
200 Madison Avenue, New York, NY 10016.
The name "BERKLEY" and the stylized "B" with design
are trademarks belonging to the Berkley Publishing Corporation.

PRINTED IN THE UNITED STATES OF AMERICA

[redacted]

7-13-87

Put God to Work . . . for You!

ALBQ

There is a God. He is with us from 9 to 5, as well as from 5 to 9. From first awakening, through the busy day, this witty, illuminating book offers meditation and guidance. Follow the clock from chapter to chapter and learn how to:

- Eliminate stress
- Improve office atmosphere and relationships
- Change perspective and alter your day
- Work more efficiently

How to Keep God Alive from 9 to 5 unequivocally shows that there is a place for God in the business world. Discover in the poems, prayers and thoughts within, new attitudes and opportunities available to all who learn to invite God into their office.

"A pithy volume of helpful hints!" —*Newsweek*

"If you have ever wondered how God and religion could possibly mix with the pulls and strains of the business world, you ought to read this book!"

—Anthony de Mello, author of *Sadhana*

"Aimed at anyone who works, and particularly those who work in a business setting, this little book has concrete suggestions for everyday situations where God can all-too-easily be ignored—or where God can be called upon for strength and served."

—*The News and Courier* (Charleston, S.C.)

For my mother and father, who introduced me to God . . . and Roseanna, who keeps reintroducing me.

CONTENTS

This book makes three assumptions. Those assumptions are:

1. There is a God.
2. He is not George Burns.
3. God works where we work.

Now the real significance of those three assumptions is:

1. That's all the assumptions we'll make.

We do not, and will not, assume that you accept, adore, or even tolerate God in any specific way. Nor do we assume that you have or have not formally enchurched God. That may be true, but that's not an assumption we make—or require—for reading on. No, we merely ask that for the following pages, and any reflection on them that gives you pause, you accept only that:

1. There is a God.
2. He is not a Hollywood creation.
3. He's with us from 9 to 5 as well as from 5 to 9.

Now that's always been the toughie for me—Assumption Three. Through the years I have had trouble accepting—or more accurately, acknowledging—the fact that God goes to work with me. I could more readily accept an actor on some late late movie claiming that God was his co-pilot than acknowledge the fact that God is my co-*worker*.

Why's that?

Well, I've struggled to come up with the reason. I've even tried, off and on, to rationalize the situation. I thought for a while that I could chalk it up to the hurly-burly of commerce, the daily distractions of business, the pace that didn't allow for alleluias and praise be's. But that would have been an all too superficial answer. Easy. Expected. And what's more, we're not talking now or anywhere else about alleluias at the water cooler and praise be's in the mailroom. We're not talking about histrionic holiness. No way. Not at all.

Then why did I have trouble with Assumption Three? Was it embarrassment? Fear? Squeamishness? Denial? Something to do with my image?

No, nothing as psychologically hip as any of those reasons. After some mulling in solitude, I concluded that my problem in acknowledging the vitality of God in my 9-to-5 life was based, purely and simply, on *responsibility*. I was uncomfortable in assuming the responsibility that comes with believing in God.

It's this way: no matter if you think of God as Creator, crutch, or crony, there is a *responsibility* in acknowledging the existence of God that goes far beyond the time being shown on your sporty digital. Acceptance of God means the presence of God—at the ungodliest hours. Now 3 A.M. has been the cliché godless hour for a long, long time. But 9 to 5 have been mentioned more and more often as godless hours as well.

But are they? Are our business hours devoid of deity, bereft of anything blessed? Are these hours really godless?

Godvoid?

Godbarred?

Obviously I don't think so.

Yet it's very tricky—heroically presumptuous, some say—to write a book on how to sacravivify one's business life. It's easy to be accused of spewing pious piffle. "Who in corporate headquarters are you, Chervokas, to be telling me about *my* spiritual life?"

"Telling?" Wrong word? Please don't misread "telling." Don't misinterpret the word. I'm telling, yes, but telling in this context should mean relating. Relating, not preaching. Portraying, not expounding.

You can watch Julia Child whip up a terrific cassoulet and although she is *telling* you all the while how to do it you can follow her recipe or not. You can alter Julia's recipe, leaving out an ingredient or tossing something you prefer into the stew. In the same way Jane Fonda can *tell* you some tummy-tightening tips and you can go halfway with Jane, the whole way, or no way at all. Similarly you can skim through John Naisbitt's megaguesses and accept them, or any one of them, or not. Yep, free will can sure be a lot of fun.

And so it is with this book. You can go through the prototypical business day that follows and see where God might rate an appearance in your business day. It might be for a fleeting tribute or a quick chat. You might choose to work some of the suggestions made into *your* day or not. Maybe you'll sense the many situations, the host of opportunities (even during the most indigo of Mondays) where God can be squeezed into your schedule. Then perhaps you'll conclude, as I did, that one can be comfortable with God from 9 to 5 without thinking himself holier than the guy in the next office—which, of course, if one does, one isn't.

There's another big—and just as beautiful—benefit in all this. Once you can admit that God and you have a pretty fair office relationship going, you might find yourself working communal wonders for your colleagues, your clients, your company, yourself. Not necessarily bottom-line wonders, not that sevenfold reward that you might have been secretly hoping for. No, rather a head and heart and soul payoff. And relief.

Relief? Yes, relief. Taking the pressure off.

Eliminating stress.

Focusing on the important.

Being tickled—not bugged—by the trivial.

Understanding your boss.

Actually liking your clients.

Not watching the clock, waiting for the day to end.

Returning home feeling good about the day—and yourself.

How in heaven's name can these good things be achieved merely by penciling in God somewhere in that 9-to-5 stretch? Let's go through a likely business day and see. Let's flip through our desk calendars and consider the opportunities to include God that we have been overlooking.

And those overlooked opportunities may start long before we get to the office.

Up and at 'Em

Chances are pretty good that once you crawl or bound out of bed you'll head for the shower. Your enthusiasm for doing so depends on your metabolism. Now, that forceful spray that comes out of the showerhead is a neat way to wash the night off your skin and the clutter out of your head. And while you're clutter-cleansing and washing away foggy dream images, you'll undoubtedly start cataloging all your scheduled confrontations of the day, the meetings and presentations and host of potential jeopardy situations that await you.

As the water perks up your pores the word "deal" may pop into your head. As in "Big deal." As in "Let's make a deal." As in "Oooo, have I got a deal for you."

It's likely that you'll hear that word more than once during the day ahead of you. Some may cringe at the word "deal." To many, "deal" is a street word. Rough, tactless, associated perhaps with mercantile machinations of a shady sort.

But not necessarily. I like the word "deal." It's a decent little word. "Deal" deserves a better reputation. We will have to deal with one another constantly throughout the day. We will have to evaluate one another's premises and conclusions, judgments and decisions. We will have to cope, to thrive, to survive, to eke, to get by, to negotiate, to cajole, to convince, to allay, to sway—to "deal."

As you grope for that soap-on-a-rope, as you fumble for the bottle of shampoo, gurgle a greeting to God. Something like this, perhaps: *"As I deal with people today, Father, let me remember how wondrously You have dealt with me."*

Give a quick and passing thought to some of the better "deals," some of the more than merely fair shakes you've gotten from God recently. Maybe you can pass along that sense of decent dealing to others along the way during the day. As you rinse the lather out of your eyes, consider that you probably can trust His judgment a lot more than you can that of the Vice President of Administration and Personnel. If you expect Him to give you a fair "deal," how about your relationship with customers and clients and fellow workers?

"As I deal with people today, Father, let me remember how wondrously You have dealt with me."

That's a snippet of a prayer, really, not much more than a hello, how-are-ya, best wishes. That's all some conversations have to be. No more than that. It's when we begin programming our would-be conversations with family and friends—and even God—that we get stuffy and stilted and, worst of all, insincere and artificial. A passing remark, a little bit of a thought is enough to establish a solid communication link. That's true for the people you work with. That's true for God.*

Now, as you step out of the shower there's every likelihood that a mirror will confront you, and, as is a mirror's quintessential wont, that mirror will probably reveal you to yourself.

Rest easy. Don't expect any saccharine reflection on reflections here. No cheap analogy—although the temptation is there and, understandably, is great. From a practical point of view (rather than the potentially tacky poetic point of view) the mirror does offer us an opportunity to get the day started in a God mode rather than in an antsy, fidgety business mode.

Think of the mirror as a mnemonic device. It should remind us of a common but significant action that we'll lapse into during the day.

Although it is still early and you haven't had your infusion of caffeine yet, look into that steamed-up bathroom mirror—and smile.

"Did the man say 'smile'? At this hour of the morning? With the way that I feel? That guy's got to be some sort of pollyannic pecan!"

Nutty idea or not, go ahead and try it. Try to smile into the mirror without feeling like a fool. No one's watching—except for Him, and He really doesn't

* (A word of explanation about God as male. I'm male. If I am truly created in God's image, God, for me, is male. If you are female, God, for you, may be female. Not wanting to get bogged down in He/She's every time God is mentioned, I'll refer to the Almighty as male. Yes, some may perfer addressing God as a Hermaphrodeity, but I'd rather not.)

care how silly your sunrise grin looks. Now, as you stand there sopping and smiling and staring into the bathroom mirror, pray something like this:

May every smile I smile today, Father
Come easily and from within;
No frozen smile
Yanked out of my psychological fridge
To be grandly, matter-of-factly
Flashed whenever I sense the need.
No, may my every smile be spontaneous,
Warm, impromptu and not politically
programmed.
Don't let me forget, Father,
Today and always,
That a smile should be
A prayer, not a pose.

Imagine if we could pull that off. Imagine if all of us could really consider our smiles to be prayers and not poses. I'll bet we could move some heretofore immovable mountains.

Too often we slip into a smile to cover up our boredom with a particular person or situation. Then, too, we smile inanely at some airhead remark or even at a matter-of-fact introduction, greeting, or good-bye. In these cases, both smile and smiler are mechanical and insincere. Willy Loman, you may recall—and hopefully shudder at the recollection—was a man "riding on a smile and a shoeshine." Maybe we can scrub our superficial smiles for prayerful ones.

That's right . . . if we could consider our smile to be a face-muscle reaction that translates into "*God bless you/God bless me,''* we would all suffer fools and painful situations much more easily, even though the fool and the cause for the pain happens to be, for the moment at least, our own assinine self.

Our smile need not be ''the chosen vehicle of all ambiguities'' as Melville suggested. Our smile can be a clear message that says:

> *Happy to be sharing humanity with you . . .*
> *Here's hoping we're doing right by God . . .*
> *And He continues to deal wondrously with us all.*

Nothing ambiguous about that. But certainly a morale booster, especially during a draggy sort of morning.

En Route

The shower and the bathroom, the solitude of the room and the rituals practiced therein, are conducive to Godthink and Godtalk. There is very little there to distract us once we get onto a channel with our Creator. But our day's distractions begin with our commute. The real concerns of our business pressures and daily dilemmas hit us full force as we're getting to the office. And what a foul full force it is!

Our transportation systems do more to squelch any and all Godthoughts than just about any other institution I can think of. Who can ponder his relationship with God when he's forced to stand and sway his way to work in an overcrowded, underventilated bus or train? What saint-in-training can chat with God in a car stuck three miles behind a fender-bending accident?

Although we might have greeted God as we dried off, there's no longer any memory of that chat once our train is at a standstill or our car's radiator is boiling over. As we agonize with our fellow commuters somewhere in that taxing transit, we leave God by the pikeside, or on a cold commuter platform, or at a bus stop.

We forget all about God—and frequently don't pick Him up until we're on our way home, moaning as we do in mock relief, "God, am I glad *this* day is over."

Isn't it inevitable? Likely, but not inevitable, because even in the hustle and hassle of going to work we can find a few seconds for a reflection on God and our relationship to Him. And, especially, our *need* for Him. Think of the brief time we all have in the morning waiting for our turn to cross at a busy intersection. Imagine saying to God:

Why is it I'll pay strict attention
To a dumb "WALK" and "WAIT" sign
But I'll balk and squawk
When someone asks me to be
A little more generous
With my life and the people in it?
Help me, Almighty God, to see
And read and respond to Your *signs,*
Signs that may not help me get across the street,
But should help me get to
That joyous eternity You promised all of us.

That prayer takes about twenty-five seconds, just about the time it takes for the light to change from stand-still red to walk-on green. You get the idea? A day is chock full of moments like this, brief periods of waiting and whiling. Those seconds of momentary inactivity are perfect for a quickie prayer, a wish or a plea.

A word here about people who are, for whatever reason, angry in the A.M. You run into them weekly, if not daily. Maybe you yourself, Mr. Hyde, are one of these early morning monsters.

The irony of it all is that many of these angry folks drive cars sporting spiritually oriented bumper stickers. I have followed a GOD LOVES YOU sign a number of times that's affixed to a car that darts in and out of lanes without signaling. The self-professed God-loving driver honks his horn wildly at cars ahead of him, and then curses out pedestrians who are distressedly caught in between light changes. I have always wanted to create a special bumper sticker to be slapped alongside this driver's GOD LOVES YOU bumper sticker. My countersticker would read HUGGED A HYPOCRITE TODAY?

It is understandable that we might be tense to the point of anger as we go off to work. Understandable, but hardly justifiable. Although a friend of mine once wove this lovely piece of sophistry: "If one of the punishments meted out to Adam and Eve for their apple-curiosity was that they had to go off and work, then work in itself must be an evil. After all, punishments aren't good things. Punishments are meant to hurt. So," continued my friend, "work is a hurtful thing and people who say they enjoy their work are actually enjoying punishment . . . and are, therefore, masochists."

Clever argument, but masochists by definition would look forward to going off to their punishwork every morning. Those iron-jawed, tight-lipped drivers sure don't look as if they're going off to a pleasurable—albeit perversely pleasurable—experience.

As you encounter en route anger in the morning, you might like to whisper this wish:

Maybe his anger stems from not knowing
what the day holds,
what the day will bring;
Quiet that anger, Father, by letting him know
that whatever the day holds,
it will always hold You.

It's still not nine and already you may have found some opportunities to chat with God that you hadn't considered before. But a word of caution. Should you adopt and use all of the suggestions made in this book, you could get the label—and justifiably so—of being a "white-collar monastic." It is not my intent to have you spend every waking working minute focused on God. Not by a long shot. The thoughts herein are for your consideration as singular ways to keep God alive in your workaday life. Lumping all those singular ways together would obviously result in one incredible super-sacred—and sanctimoniously silly—day. No. Rather, pick and choose. Try one or two that seem right for you. Overlook any suggestion that you just wouldn't feel comfortable with.

Almost There

As you debark, alight, bolt out of whatever vehicle that's taking you to work, there's a good chance that someone will wish you—or you will wish someone—"Have a nice [or good] day." Depending on your mood of the moment, you may smile (a pose or a prayer?) or wince. You may reciprocate or regurgitate. There's no question that "Have a nice day" is overused—and therefore a fairly innocuous, if not meaningless, expression. But have you considered trying to come up with pertinent substitutes for the expression? Not even for the whole expression, just for the word "nice" or the word "good"?

Have you tried to find a word that's especially appropriate for the person you're saying it to, at the particular time you're saying it? Like "have a *dry* day" to an umbrellaless person on a misty morning. Or to the office jock—"have a *World Class* day." Or to the office Nervous Nellie—"have a *mellow* day.'' To a stockbroker—''have an *up* day.'' Use adjectives, where they are appropriate, like ''quiet,'' ''steady,'' ''swift,'' ''sweet,'' ''loving,'' ''easy,'' ''hopeful,'' ''heroic'' and even, if the spirit so moves you, ''blessed.'' In short, give some sort of dimension to a person's day-wish.

Now what does this have to do with God?

It's a little way of telling God (and one more way of including Him in your business day) that you care enough about your God-sprung brothers and sisters (His creations too, after all) to wish them a specific wish, to be sensitive to their special needs.

By personalizing your day-wish to your commuting friends and passing acquaintances you're saying something about our communal humanity, our shared dignity, and our real need for mutual respect.

As for that dignity . . . It's sure not easy maintaining it a minute or two before nine as you elevate, escalate, or tromp up to your place of business. You're shoulder to shoulder, body to body, pressed against flesh just as apprehensive about the day ahead as you may be.

My office is on the sixteenth floor, which certainly affords me a spectacular view but getting there isn't always half the fun. Or *any* fun. The elevator, more often than not, stops at every other floor, opening up its welcoming doors time and again to even more incoming flesh. How can the thought of God squeeze into this up-and-down sardine can? By calling out to Him this way:

You've asked us to touch one another with love.
And we should. And we shall.
But for now it's shoulders and hips and elbows

That are touching, pressing, rubbing
Up against bodies they've never been introduced to.
Bless all these bodies, Lord, casually congested.
Bless the spirits within, that we may realize
Our obligation to touch one another's lives,
If not this literally,
Certainly lovingly.
Amen.

Although that conversation with God first appeared in my book *Pinstripe Prayers,* I'm including it here to underscore a point about people we don't know. Unless we are forest rangers, shepherds or lighthouse keepers, we will run into—literally and figuratively—hundreds of people on any given business day. These people may be in crowded elevators, on congested street corners, in jam-packed cafeterias.

Consider that a brief prayer for a stranger strolling along wearing a deeply imbedded scowl just might work wonders. A brief prayer like:

Bless her and her life;
Give her,
If it's Your will,
A double order of Your consolation

for a bag lady you come across will do both of you a world of good.

"Peace and a kind day to all of us" is a lovely way to pray for all of you lined up in the pouring rain waiting for a bus.

What a marvelous feeling to realize that we're in

this thing of Life together. All of us are. You. Me. And Him.

Ever consider prayerful reciprocity? Quick little prayers for people we see once, and probably never again? Imagine millions of us praying for each other as we walk down the street, climb stairs, sit on park benches.

Today or tomorrow pick out a face in the crowd and spontaneously wish to God for something for that person. And then, if you're of a mind and can program your memory, mentally hark back to that person a couple of times during the course of the day, recalling something about the person's face and expression. Now, could you ever bring yourself to think that that person is as important to you as your spouse or child or parent? Oooo, that's tough. That's almost impossible. That's the stuff of saints. But wouldn't it be something if we all could think that much of one another? Of one, just one, stranger every day?

Starting Time

Starting Time, no matter what the sign-in sheet or the punch clock says, is not always the moment one begins to work. More often it's the time one begins the ritual that leads to work. The ritual that leads to work is not part of the job. The ritual's not in your job description. So what's the ritual?

Ritual*s*, really. Different rites for different folks. Here are the most common Starting Time rituals:

- finishing the crossword puzzle at your desk that you had started on the train.
- doing your makeup.
- relating last night's episode of the blockbuster miniseries to someone who'll relate back to you the last three innings of last night's ball game.
- getting out of your running shoes and into your office shoes (a rather new ritual—and one that I find intriguing).

- calling home with reminders of things to be done by members of the family who were still asleep when you left for work.
- making lunch plans.

Now, all those rituals have as their premise the company owing its employees a warm-up time, of sorts—a limbering up before plunging ahead with the day's work. That may or may not be true; this is not a treatise on employee-management relations. The point is that some people do feel the need to ease into work rather than plunge into work. Easing in, of course, gives us a better opportunity to have a Godthought (while applying eyeliner or struggling to come up with a four-letter word for "Hawaiian goose"). Work-plungers, on the other hand, tend to bury themselves in the day's business activities right away.

For work-plungers (I'm one), God is tougher to think of, tougher to occupy a top-of-mind position. On the other hand, by the time you have figured out that "nene" is the word for "Hawaiian goose" you have probably invoked the name of God a few times already, but not necessarily in a prayerful sense.

There's another distraction associated with Starting Time that merits mention. It certainly gets our attention. That's checking out how people look.

When nine o'clock rolls around and the staff comes rolling in, haven't you caught yourself eyeballing employees to see what they're wearing, what they've done to their hair, how and where they got that terrific tan?

"What's with the suspenders, Sean?"

"You weren't a blonde Friday, were you, Mary Jane?"

"Bahamas for the weekend, Donna? With who?"

These are a few examples of showing interest in people (good) but needling them (not so good). Yes, we did notice something about the people, and we did make it clear to them that we noticed. But in the way we couched our Starting Time observations we may have weakened, not strengthened, our mutual-respect relationship with those people.

There's another plus for us work-plungers: we are either so into our work, or so insensitive to hairstyles and such, that we never check out how people look. Is that really a plus? Or a minus?

Let's think about that—over coffee.

COFFEE

Coffee commercials have implanted the thought in our heads that sharing a cup of coffee makes us friendlier, more sensitive people. We welcome friends, neighbors, strangers, even mothers-in-law into our kitchens (in commercials, at least) to quaff a mug of java with us.

In the office, however, the situation is not quite the same. A whopping percentage of us are not at the coffee wagon, at the coffee machine, in the coffee line—but we *are* drinking coffee. And we are drinking coffee because we sent someone *else* to get it for us.

For many of us the ordering of and the getting of coffee is the first boss/bossed manifestation of the business day. And it can set the wrong tone for the rest of the day.

Oh, we might be courteous (?) enough to say something like, "I'll have a regular and maybe half a bagel, butter, no cream cheese.'' And even politely (?) add, ''Oh, yes—and bring it into Conference Room A . . . please.'' But what does all this coffee assertiveness say about our humanity, do for our humanity? Before we bark for coffee—or before we grumblingly shuffle off to fetch a cup for the aforementioned, expletive-deleted barker—let's talk the whole situation over with God.

Prayer of Someone Ordering Coffee

Remind me, God, as I ask her for coffee
That soft-spoken respect
Should accompany my every request.
If I'd stop and think twice
About snapping at You
When I ask You *for a favor,*
Why shouldn't I do the same
When I ask a favor of her?

Prayer of Someone Getting Coffee

Remind me, God, that going for coffee
Isn't such a heroic chore
Nor a monumental trip.
But remind him, too, God,
That though our Job Titles are different,
In Your eyes our Life Titles are one and the same.
Now, if You can get
That message across to him, Father,
Who knows—
Maybe someday
He'll go and get coffee for me.

The coffee cup could well be your first business prop (see "Godprops" at 11:20) of the day. It may be a paper, plastic, or Styrofoam prop. Or it may be a ceramic prop that says to your make-a-buck world "I love New York," "Greatest Daddy in the World," "Caffeine Addict" or "Edna."

What are *you* saying with your coffee container?

I've thought about the things I may have been saying, wittingly or unwittingly, with a cup of coffee throughout my business career. My mug and I have spoken volumes—and not necessarily the nicest of volumes either. Here are some of the things coffee and I have said:

- "We're important, very important. Look at the way we sip before we speak. The way we pause, take a gulp and resume speaking. That's power, folks—and you'd better appreciate it."
- "We're thoughtful, we're intelligent. Look at the way we lean back and put cup to lip, letting the warmth trickle into our learned mouths. Aren't we smart?"
- "Wow! Are we hung over! Let's down the first cup in a hurry and keep 'em coming. That was some night. But look what it says about dynamic us that we can party all night and still be at the job at nine the next morning."
- "We're frightened. Scared stiff. The cup is our bolster, quite literally our prop. The new client looks like a mean so-and-so, but he'll never suspect we are in awe of him if we sit here and sip in feigned confidence."
- "You're a jerk, a wimp. Can't you see that we, cup and I, know you're full of baloney. You go

on with your dumb presentation and we sip with a sneer, almost chuckling behind the rim of this hefty, heavy, manly mug.''

And these are just a few of the things I can recall coffee and me saying, which is to say we should be more circumspect about our communication. Sure, nobody *heard* our words. But they *felt* them. They felt them because of the way we handled our coffee, waved our coffee, sipped our coffee out of that oversized mug with ''BOSS'' embossed on it.

We'll run into, grope, and fondle other business props during this day, but for now let's recall that in our hands every one of those props has a symbolic language all its own. We can make props like the coffee mug say almost anything we choose. So we should choose our prop language as carefully as we select our spoken language.

Dignity. Respect. Shared humanity. Prop language and spoken language can exalt them or dishonor them. It's our call.

First Meeting of the Day

The first meeting of the day, if it wasn't a breakfast meeting held earlier (breakfast meetings are a recent business phenomenon that we are overlooking in this prototypical day . . . just as we always overlook eggs Benedict when they are served at such a meeting) will probably be a group meeting of some kind. The meeting may be labeled any number of things: General Staff Meeting, Operations Committee Meeting, Weekly Department Update, Sales Forecast Conference or some such handle.

But the commonality of all these first gatherings of the day, whatever they are called, is that they are *big* meetings. Not big in the sense of importance—big in the sense of attendance. They are large meetings because someone wants to be sure as many people get in on time, or as nearly on time, as possible.

Although the 9:30 meeting may not be important

in that no cataclysmic announcements will be made nor any weighty corporate decisions revealed, it does give the numerous attendees a chance to make their individual presence known, if so desired. And a lot of us so desire.

The 9:30 meeting is our first major, scheduled opportunity of the day to exercise our ego. Even more noteworthy, it's an opportunity to exercise our ego in front of a wonderfully varied audience. Very often this meeting will include not only our peers, but our superiors and inferiors as well. Peers, superiors, and inferiors on the corporate chart, that is. And *only* on the corporate chart, let's hope.

How you choose to exercise your ego in this situation is, of course, up to you. Among your many options may be delivering a snappy report on your department's successful office-supply austerity program . . . or an incisive question asked of the personnel director concerning minority hiring . . . or an impromptu thought on a possible way to boost sagging sales in the Southwest region. Whatever your choice, you know when you're making that early morning contribution that a dozen or more sets of eyes are focused on you. And you love it.

And there is absolutely nothing wrong, nothing guilt-riddling about loving it. An ego can be a beautiful thing. I don't know what the expression "healthy ego" does for our language except to point to a "diseased ego." I prefer to refer to a "beautiful ego" which implies that in its "beauty" an ego reflects and is reflected by the goodness of the world around it.

Long before *I* felt good about ego, Sherwood Anderson felt good about it. And he wrote good things about it—in his *Memoirs.* "What's wrong with this egotism?" said Anderson. "If a man doesn't delight in himself and the force in him and feel that he and it are wonders, how is all life to become important to him? The interest in the lives of others, the high evaluation of these lives, what are they but the overflow of the interest he finds in himself, the value he attributes to his own being?"

As well as getting a vigorous, head-shaking, brain-rattling nod from me, Anderson's thought is notable for a couple of words contained therein. The words are "delight" and "force."

We have been told since time immemorial to "delight in Him." I translate this exhortation to mean "feel confident," almost cocky, a bit feisty, knowing that you and God have some kind of relationship going.

Delight that God is in your conference room.

Delight that He's in the audience as you are exercising your ego.

Delight that *He has dealt wondrously with you.* That's egotism—a beautiful egotism. What's wrong with it? Nothing. Absolutely nothing.

As for the word "force," it may have grown a little stale since *Star Wars.* But trite or not, whatever "force" we can attribute as being with us, knowing that it is there gives us a daily confidence boost that smacks of egotism. That confidence can take us through the day and through a lifetime if we keep on feeding, nurturing it, giving it daily workouts.

That confidence can certainly take us through the early morning meeting. And give the rest of the day a "delightful" sort of impetus.

Annoying Phone Calls

Some of us who are congenitally uncomfortable with Mr. Bell's brainchild might consider *every* phone call to be irritating. Nevertheless, certain calls can be more annoying than others because of the content of the call, the caller, or the inappropriate time of the call.

At face (of-the-clock) value, the 9:58 call may not be that untimely. After all, being told of an incoming call while you are addressing the Operations Committee can send a message to the group that you are very, very important—and so you leave the meeting to take the call flashing a bit of a self-satisfied grin on your corporate kisser. (Grins aren't prayers; smiles are.) Ah, but then when you get to the phone and find that the call is from some anonymous mutual funds solicitor you are genuinely—and for my money, justifiably—bugged.

Irritating calls of a similar nature may come from

suppliers asking you for "ten minutes . . . just ten minutes of your time," from job seekers, employment agents wondering if you are totally happy in your present position, survey-takers, and old college chums "just passing through town."

How do you handle such calls?

Have you noticed how much easier it is to be rude to someone over the phone than to someone in person? The things you say to a person over the phone can be cutting, vicious, ugly. Given the same situation, but having the person standing across the desk from you, you would never think of being so acerbic. Remote rudeness, for many, is a business way of life. But it doesn't have to be.

I don't hold Alexander Graham Bell in as much esteem as I do the anonymous genius who came up with the idea of the "hold" button. Consider that invention. Not only is it a wonderful device to use to get your anger under control, but the "hold" button also gives you a chance to check in with God during an especially annoying call.

Say to the pushy caller on the phone, "Just hold for a few seconds . . . I'll get right back to you." And while the person is holding, you say to God:

Teach me to be patient, God,
With my brothers and sisters
Who don't deserve to be lambasted or sassed;
Teach me to be patient
And decent and civil,
Yes, teach me to be patient—but teach me fast!

Whether patience can be achieved all that quickly, I don't really know. I *do* know, however, that in the mere plea for patience there is an acknowledgment that we don't have patience, could use patience, and should work on developing it. After that kind of wrenching avowal to God, we might even return to our investment-counseling pest and say something uncharacteristically nice like, "I appreciate your interest but I have all the financial guidance I need right now. Thank you so much. Good-bye and good luck."

Kind. Courteous. Not overly congenial. Just right. And *almost* sincere!

The Mail

Anticipation can make a person's day. Anticipation can also keep some people alive. A study of centenarians has revealed that those very very senior citizens who have something to look forward to—say, a visit from a niece six months hence—remain healthier, more resolute, and generally tend to go on living, whereas centenarians with nothing to look forward to tend to wind down their lives rather abruptly.

On a somewhat less life-threatening level, the anticipation of the morning mail can have a salubrious effect on certain members of the work force. And, it follows, a not so salubrious effect on others.

I look forward to mail in the office as much as any child at camp looks forward to a package from home. And just what are *my* chocolate-chip cookies?

A whole host of goodies like trade magazines and call reports and résumés and requests for speaking engagements. I find them all interesting in one way or another, even those scraps of mail that ask me to join, to subscribe, to contribute, to protest, to—whatever.

Anticipation need not presume anxiety, although there are still, even in these supposedly enlightened corporate times, folks who are concerned about finding a pink slip in their morning mail. Anticipation is a wonder, a blessing, a good.

If you, as a part of your job duties, have to open someone else's mail for them, do you share in the anticipation and its requitedness or unrequitedness? And do you, who have your mail opened for you, share your feelings about that mail with your secretary?

At camp the kids, some more grudgingly than others to be sure, share their chocolate-chip cookies. In the armed forces guys pass around clippings and pictures sent from home. In business, although the anticipation may be there we tend to be private about it—and about where that anticipation may lead.

Anticipation is at the heart of one's Godlife. Anticipating a wonderful today, a marvelous tomorrow, and a joyous forever. Anticipating a reply from your new business mailing can give you some indication as to what a human hoot this particular facet of 9-to-5 life can be. Looking forward to things as seemingly trivial as the morning mail can make life much more intriguing, not merely for centenarians, but even for all our hustling YUPPIE friends in the office.

That's why when we are on the sending end of a mailing piece we should do our utmost to care, really care. In the creation of a business letter we should remember that we are sending it to a brother or sister, not to a cold computer or a paragon of robotic science. We should be human in our written communications and not merely dash off a few thoughtless paragraphs in the lingo of our profession, in a letter riddled with whatever clichés our particular industry has grown wallowingly accustomed to. If we can remember that the receiver of our letter is an Anticipator like us, we might take more pains with our prose. And we should. We really should.

That holds true for internal office memos as well. Whether you are in a position of writing them, receiving them, or just slinging them from one desk to another, remember that the memos are thoughts, and alleged feelings, of one Godwrought being to another—or maybe even a committee of Godwrought beings. (It's a constant consolation to me to realize that although God created man and woman there is no recorded testimony that He created committees. For this alone we should worship Him.)

No matter how we choose to communicate with one another—on paper, by phone, or in person—and no matter what our particular pet anticipation might be, we should all be able to anticipate—and expect—kindness from one another.

UNKINDNESS

Absolutely no available statistics, just plain old observation, reveal that more people work for Hardnose & Bottomline than work for Utopia, Inc. And no matter how successful corporate culture-shapers are in trying to create a pleasant ambience at Hardnose & Bottomline, there's bound to be a person or six there who are *un*pleasant. Some of these people are unpleasant by nature, others are unpleasant by circumstance. And still others go beyond unpleasant—all the way to un*kind*. Now just what kinds of unkindnesses might you run up against at the office? Many kinds, the most notable of which are these:

—*Ethnic nastiness*. In the last decade we have taken an ugly leap from the innocuous hokum of Pat and Mike jokes and Max and Sol gags. Yes, ethnic humor of a generation or two ago was focused on stereotypes, but the humor was gentle and mild, rarely biting. Today's ethnic humor, however, slashes mercilessly and, after the slashing, goes ahead and sprinkles salt into the wounds. Today's ethnic humor is hurtful and insidious. Yet what is our reaction to it? What happens when the guy in the adjacent office rushes in with "Hey, have you heard the one about the Italian bowling team that . . ."? How will we react? What, if anything, will we say?

—*Putdown zingers.* What hath Don Rickles wrought? The comics whose routines are based on running down people have been a source of inspiration to hundreds of amateur wags. Our children's humor has become intensely personal and pointed. Street humor is a raging, ragging thing in which even someone's mother is fair game. Office humor is built on the client's drinking, the personnel lady's big nose, the research director's lisp, anyone's baldness, weakness, or uniqueness.

An associate of mine who otherwise seems to be a charitable and considerate soul has a propensity to put down people who tend to be overweight. After months of hearing him say things like "Check out the hefty hoofs of Margie down in accounting" and "You know what they say, Sam, two chins are better than one" I asked my colleague why he was compelled to comment so critically about people's weight. He was rather surprised at my question and answered, "Hell, John, at least it shows that I notice them."

"Yeah, but . . ." I never finished my "Yeah, but . . ." because, although my friend's solution was a little perverse, the thought struck me that one of the worst forms of office unkindness is . . .

—*Disregard.* A secretary sends you a suggestion for a new, faster time-sheet system and you totally disregard the suggestion. A person reporting to you asks for "ten minutes of your time whenever it's convenient" in order to chat about his career growth opportunities at the firm and you never get back to him. A list of "please return call" memos (see 2:05) from last Friday sits on your desk untouched, undialed, on Tuesday morning. Why? "Completely slipped my mind?" "Didn't really seem important?" "Busy right now . . . intend to respond later?" Are those excuses real—or flimsy rationales?

Can we imagine how the people we are disregarding feel about the neglect we're showing? André Gide could and did and wrote: "True kindness presupposes the faculty of imagining as one's own the sufferings and joy of others. Without imagination, there can be weakness, theoretical or practical philanthropy, but not true kindness." Or, in homier terms, put yourself in the other guy's shoes.

—*Mean-spiritedness*. The prior three forms of unkindness can often be chalked up to simple carelessness, thoughtlessness—and thus can be remedied without too much wrenching of spirit and soul. But there are some officemates who seem to be irreparable knockers, putting down everything and everybody. Their dispositions are out-and-out rotten. Their meanness is not wrapped in humor, even derogatory humor; it is just oblivious uncaring. They seem to go out of their way to spread their rottenness. What can we do about this sort of person? What can we do that even a shrink might have difficulty doing? We can smile at him or her. Yes, simply smile. Not a derisive smile or a condescending smile. A *serene* smile, which, after all, is a prayer. Every time that mean-spirited stinker tears something down we can smile and say something like, "Not really," or "I don't see it that way," or "Why did you say that?" Or simply smile and say nothing at all. Smile and walk away to some other activity. Smile and perhaps say to that other business colleague of yours, God:

May I meet meanness
Not with anger,
But with blessed forbearance,
Forbearance—one more gift
From Your boundless store of gifts.

May my smile
Send out a signal
That there is peace for troubled spirits,
Peace—the greatest *gift*
Of all your wondrous gifts.

The Interview

Some of the value judgments we must make on a business morning have very little cosmic importance. Sure, we may find choosing between Italian and Chinese for lunch a bit of a kick, but deciding whether to go for manicotti or moo goo gai pan is hardly as monumental an undertaking as, say, deciding on a person's career.

There is probably no more "boy-do-I-wish-this-were-over" appointment for the day than a job interview (unless it's firing someone—see 4:30). And that goes for both the interviewer as well as the interviewee. At least it's so for *this* interviewer. Somewhere out there maybe there's a person who actually enjoys interviewing another person. But I'm not the guy.

Once a person's skills have been established and corroborated (with tests or references or what have you), the point of an interview is to probe the applicant's personality, character, interests, energy level, ambition, neatness. I don't relish any of that. I don't like it done to me; I don't like to do it unto others.

Still, it's the business way of life. To my knowledge nothing better has come along. No one has devised "character sensors" that we can apply to a person's body to get a quick and accurate impression of that person. No "laser ambition scans" to give us a read on an applicant's hungriness. No, nothing like that yet. For a half hour or so we play, verbally and alone, detective, psychologist, confessor, sociologist and occasionally—*sorry about that, God*—God.

How uncomfortable am I, the interviewer, in interview situations? Well, as soon as I ask the applicant to take a seat (which more often than not is on a sofa so plush that she sinks into it and finds it impossible to maintain any seated dignity), I—I the purportedly in-control interviewer—begin to feel moisture collecting under my button-down oxford cloth.

Nevertheless there is a lesson to be learned in an uncomfortable interview situation. At least there is for me, and perhaps for you too. It's that although we must, it seems, constantly prove our worth to one another, person to person, one to one, God never asks us to prove our worth to Him. His acceptance of us is total, unconditional, which should alleviate if not our physical perspiration, certainly any psychological sweat we may be feeling.

Then, too, if we understand that God doesn't demand any character references of us, we may be much less apprehensive about character probing the person enveloped in our floppy sofa.

It's the same we're-in-this-thing-together notion I mentioned some time before. Once we are honest enough to accept each other's humanity, honest enough to acknowledge the strained modus operandi of the interview, we can get on with the business of business in a less stilted, more understanding and therefore kinder way.

That's where God pops up again, if we ask Him to. He can pop up as a learning aid, a guide to understanding and appreciating one another. So I look at the woman across from me and screw up my courage and candor to say to God:

Her nervousness unnerves me—
She crosses and uncrosses her legs;
Tugs at her hem,
Brushes back her hair
And speaks so fast
That I find myself speaking faster in return.

Refresh my memory, Father
So that I may hark back
To the nervousness I felt
When I was being interviewed way back when.

Grant me too the vision, Dear God,
To find, beyond her fidgets,
Talent and intelligence
That transcend the tension—
Talent and intelligence
That, once discovered, just may
Land her the job she's suffering for.

Where's Charley?

It begins innocently enough. You need some information that you know one of your associates will have at his fingertips. So you ring Charley's extension. And Charley's secretary answers, phumpheringly, ". . . er . . . ah . . . he isn't in yet."

Not in? At 10:50? Maybe he has a business appointment out of the office or maybe he's hung up in some sort of epic, history-making traffic jam. No matter. You forget about it and get your information from fingertips other than Charley's.

Some time later Charley's overly solicitous secretary calls you back and says, "Is there anything *I* can do for you, Mr. Chervokas? You see, Charley is taking a sick day today. You see, he's drained—mentally drained."

Earlier, when you learned that Charley wasn't in, you were just a little puzzled, a smidge curious as to where he could be. But now that his secretary tells you of Charley's appropriated sick day you're miffed, annoyed, bordering on going into a certifiable snit. Sick day? *Sick day?* Charley decides to take a sick day and doesn't phone in until midmorning! And what is this "mentally drained" baloney? How did we work ourselves into this tradition that presumes we can take sick days willy-nilly, that these bonus days are our due whether, in fact, we are actually ill or not?

"Mentally drained?" Mentally drained from what? From a night out with the client? From some stress getting that marketing plan out by last Friday? From a need for eighteen holes to get those long irons in shape?

Somewhere in the midst of my fuming about Charley a part of me asks just what am I getting so riled up about. Isn't Charley doing what our unwritten company policy—and hundreds of company policies—say he can be doing? So why do I think that he's cheating the firm and, in the process, doing *me* a personal wrong?

Situations like this—for me, and I would guess for a good many other people—are difficult to deal with. That's because we're confronted with two questions, two problems.

1. Is what Charley doing ethical?
2. Is it my place to be concerned about it?

As for the first question, the whole business of sick days presumes you can be ill a certain number of days a year on company time and on company pay. And, to your way of thinking, if the company nurtures that belief, well, doggone it, you will make *sure* you are sick all those days allotted you. If not actually sick, at least you'll claim to be sick. But mentally sick? How about mentally sick? Can we hedgers even hedge that far? Sure we can. If our company acquiesces or doesn't question the reason for our purported sickness, then the practice must be ethical. Mustn't it?

A survey dealing with "ethics on the job" that appeared in the August 1984 edition of *Glamour* magazine listed this question: *"Is it unethical to call in sick if you're 'mentally tired' but not physically ill?"* Only 25 percent said "Yes, it *is* unethical," and a whopping 75 percent said "No, it's *not* unethical." In fact, one respondent is quoted as saying, "I'm a firm believer in 'mental health' days." When I return to work after taking one my mind is so clear I can get twice as much done as usual."

Well, now, if Charley and the *Glamour* respondent and 75 percent of us believe it's not unethical to take a day off for the sake of our heads, why—as my second question suggests—should I care an ethical fig if we take those days off?

In fact, if a *mental health* day is perfectly permissible, I have a thought that we might all profit by occasionally taking a *spiritual health* day. And what exactly is a spiritual health day? What would one be like?

Maybe something like this:

A spiritual health day need not, and probably should not, be a retreat into whatever "desert" you find within hermetic hailing distance of your home. Historically—and all too poetically—people have thought that to be deeply in communion with the Creator they had to go to a beach, up a mountain, or into a forest. Some have done that, and have communed beautifully. But there's another way. Perhaps even a better way. Certainly, a different way.

A spiritual health day is a day when you blithely put aside every familial and personal and, of course, corporate (that's why you're getting the day off in the first place) care and plug yourself into God. Just God. God alone. No one else. Sure the idea is naïve. But then again, isn't the idea of heaven sort of naïve too?

And where do you spend your spiritual health day if not on a neighboring mountaintop? My favorite spots are not the peaceful white-sound locales like crashing-wave beaches and whistling-wind hills. No, I prefer cacophonous places, boisterously loud sites that are filled with the sounds of creation. Like a zoo, or an airport, or a train station, or a stadium. I prefer places where people and animals and machines clang and shout their sounds of being, roaring as they revel in their existence.

And as you sit or stroll through this spiritual health day you almost mindlessly permit all sorts of stimuli to bombard your senses. So keep a notebook handy. Not to transcribe any deathless prose or poetry. Keep a notebook handy to jot down words, phrases, stream-of-consciousness stuff that will invariably intrude upon whatever wavelength God and you have established for the day. Yes, it will happen. It's inevitable.

As you proceed through this spiritual health day, don't neglect your body. No, there's no need to fast. On the contrary, eat well. Go to a better restaurant, sit and gawk as you talk to God, take notes (when appropriate), take a glass of wine (always appropriate), putting yourself in His care with an almost lilies-of-the-field-like abandon.

Walk a lot, if you are able. Walking should be a big part of your spiritual health day. Not walking with any particular destination in mind. Rather, *aimless* walking. If you're walking in a city merely follow whatever light is green, crossing streets and avenues without any attention to direction, but with a great deal of attention to the sounds that come from the traffic and the scurrying people.

In a suburban setting walk through shopping centers and supermarkets, department stores and schoolyards, parking lots and playgrounds. All this uncharted strolling gives you an opportunity to wrap yourself up in a shamelessly unsophisticated awe of the concern God has for you and those widely and wildly diverse creatures around you.

A spiritual health day, ironically enough, should be a long and exhausting day. It should take you to sunset (an old reliable, if cornball, manifestation of God's wonder) and beyond. For many, the cover of night, with no sun to light up what they consider to be distractions, is even a better spiritual venue. And for others, rain is a spiritual refresher—walking in it, whistling in it, praying in it.

Finally, remember you don't have to tell Personnel that your sick day was a spiritual health day. You might have trouble, glib soul though you may be, explaining to Personnel that "No, I'm not a holy kook—a 'spiritual health day' is actually a day of *total* renewal. My mind feels better . . . my body feels better . . . all of me feels better." You might choose to paraphrase, or lift verbatim, the words of that *Glamour* survey respondent: "When I return to work . . . I can get twice as much done as usual." Should you care to explain yourself to Personnel, a promise of increased productivity never fails to impress.

RESERVATIONS

It's that time of day. Time to reach for your little black book or turn to the Rolodex or pull out once again "The Knowledgeable World's Unchallenged Guide to the Poshest Premier Eateries."

Yes, it's time to make reservations for lunch—a tough part of the day no matter what the situation, but especially tricky when you've made a lunch date with a VIBA.

A who?

A VIBA—a Very Important Business Associate.

Now who falls into that category? Who can be considered a VIBA? Well, a VIBA can be a person in your own company or someone in a similar company or in an allied, but important-to-you, industry. A VIBA may be your client. Then again you may be a VIBA's client (making you a VIBA yourself). Whatever the case, sitting down to breadsticks and a bowl of radishes with a VIBA, you think, is another one of those make-an-impression situations—so the choice of restaurant is critical to the success of the meal and/or deal. Critical? Well yes, I always thought so. And so did and do many many people like me.

It's no secret that between 9 and 5 many of us are concerned with making statements about ourselves. They don't have to be oral statements either. We make statements with things we wear, carry . . . *and eat!* In fact, we are so nutsy about these statements that we often camouflage our wonderful humanity behind these statements, these bogus badges of ours.

I have to fight the "statement sham" myself every day. Especially when it comes to selecting a restaurant. As a supercilious jerk—in the very recent past—I have been heard to say, "I will never set foot in a restaurant that has a salad bar." I have also been overheard—to my chagrin, yes, but a temporary chagrin—making reservations under the moniker Dr. Chervokas. When asked by a colleague who overheard me, "Doctor? Did you say Doctor Chervokas?" I didn't bat an eyelash. I explained to my business buddy that when one makes a reservation with "doctor" in front of one's name, the person is seated immediately and served immediately, the establishment believing that the doctor may be called out for an emergency operation at any time. Yep. Uh-huh. Yessiree. I really believed that. I really believed what I was saying.

That's why, as I now flip through my dog-eared copy of " . . . Poshest Premier Eateries" I say to God:

Keep me, Good Guardian,
Aware of myself—

So that when I feel the urge
To impress those around me,
A better part of me will tell me to stop.
May I always remember
That Your beings are treasured
For their goodness and humanity,
Not for their ability
To handle a twenty-page wine list.
Amen.

PLOTTING

Has something like this ever been said (in hushed tones or behind closed doors) to you? "Have you noticed that the work coming out of Helen's group hasn't been all that great in the past few months? Whaddayasay we, you and I, make a play for some of Helen's business—get some of her accounts shifted over to *our* group? Whaddayasay? Whaddayasay?"

Well, what *do* you say? What is your response when a colleague, a partner, a friend suggests you join forces to help out each other's career (a possibility) by giving someone else's career (quite probably) a lethal blow? Is your response likely to be one of these pips?

- "Yeah . . . Helen would probably do the same to us if we were screwing up . . . so, yeah . . . let's do it."

- "I wouldn't want to hurt Helen for the world, but for the sake of the company we probably should take over much of her business—we really should, you know, for the company's sake."
- "Sure. She'd probably welcome it—looks like she's about to snap any day now."

Among God's many bestowals upon us is that dubious one of rationalization. Sure separates us from the beasts and the birds, doesn't it? In fact, some of us are World Class rationalizers, coming up with the dandiest, most stunningly creative reasons why our actions are perfectly justifiable.

There is nothing essentially wrong, please understand, with being ambitious. It's not only our nature, it's endemic to a 9-to-5 life. In a Prayer for The Ambitious, I once wrote:

Bless us, Good God, and our earthly ambitions,
Giving us the courage and wisdom we need
To be able to recognize the difference
Between ambition—and just plain greed.

In the above example, making a play for Helen's accounts, whether that play is overt or covert, is *not* an example of out-and-out greed. No, it's a manifestation of ambition, corporate ambition—but ambition that's making its way down a pretty dirty, dingy avenue; ambition that's feeding off a human weakness.

Ambition is, or should be, at the root of every business day. That's why we are at the office in the first place. The ambition that leads us to work for a better, more comfortable, freer life for ourselves and/or any loved ones . . . the ambition that impels us to use our talents to grow and prove our mortal worth to ourselves and others (mortal worth as differentiated from *im*mortal worth, which requires no proving whatsoever) . . . the ambition that churns up our adrenaline.

Where there is *no* ambition there is boredom, joylessness, kvetching, and thirty-five hours a week of foot dragging and clock watching. Where there is *no* ambition there is dreariness of the soul.

So it's not an aberration to look at Helen's accounts and Helen's poor performance of late and, flashing the ambition that you are wearing all too visibly on your sleeve, agree to go after Helen's accounts and, consequently, Helen's livelihood. No, it's not an aberration—but it's a lousy reflection on you. Helen is not the only one who deserves better from you. So does God.

There *is* a better way to fulfill your ambition, and without stomping on Helen. That's *helping* Helen—and, coincidentally, helping yourself.

Emerson wrote, "Make yourself necessary to somebody. Do not make life hard to any." By making yourself necessary to Helen, by offering to help her *with* her accounts (rather than helping yourself *to* her accounts) you can probably further your career as you are furthering your reputation.

I say "probably" because there's always the chance that your offer to help may be misinterpreted by (a) Helen and (b) your colleagues. Unless you present your offer to help most carefully and tactfully, (a) Helen might be defensive or hurt. She could feel that her capabilities are being questioned, her territory invaded. And (b) your colleagues may think of you as some sort of corporate bleeding heart. After all, people don't go around helping one another in competitive situations, some will say. You'll have to put up with the barking of those who espouse the dog-eat-dog philosophy.

That's why, after you ixnay any sleazy thought of plotting and decide to help Helen, you might mention how you feel to God:

You can see, Almighty Father, that I'm anxious
About showing concern for someone
Who isn't linked to me by blood or love.
Quell that anxiety,
Relieve my uneasiness;
By letting me understand that,
Yes, she is *linked to me,*
And by the most magnificent connection of all—
Being.
Seeing that connection, Lord,
May I work to help her
And everyone
Who shares
That wonder of
Being.
Amen.

Godprops

Even in the most frenzied exec's day there comes a time of blessed nothingness. These are the few moments when the phone isn't ringing, the troops aren't howling, neither the sheriff nor the wolf is at the door. How fleeting are these moments? Oh, they can be as brief as twenty seconds or as long as ten minutes. You can have just enough free time to reset your calendar watch which says Wednesday instead of the Tuesday that it really is, or you can take a full ten minutes to catch a refreshing catnap.

But, if you are fortuitously given an undetermined period of time—say, because the appointment scheduled to arrive five minutes ago still hasn't shown up and you have no idea how much longer you'll have to wait—you can finger one of your Godprops and meditate on it.

That's right—Godprops. Those of us who have had to work hard at accepting God-at-work never realized all the reminders of God's office presence that are there within our reach. When we eventually stumbled upon one of these Godprops on our desk, lo and behold, there was another Godprop close by . . . and another . . . and yet another.

Just what are some of these meditation-aids, these Godprops? Why, they are things as childishly simple as—*a rubber band.* Flick a rubber band and recall that the Creator made us such resilient creatures that we are able to snap back from momentary adversity, capable of giving, of slacking off when it's called for, yet able to remain taut and resolute when that is what is needed.

Then there is the *desk calendar,* a Godprop that constantly pricks our conscience. How many of those days, that thick wad of gratuitously given time, have we frittered away, accomplishing little or nothing for whatever sphere of humanity our life impinges upon? As we flip through the days of the year remaining, can we be confident of our future, confident that we will use the time remaining—or a good part of it—to work wonders? Maybe we should shove the calendar into the musty unprobed recesses of a drawer? Or—or use it as a Gregorian goose, spurring us on to join our lives with other lives in behalf of a better life for everyone.

How about the *paper clip* as a Godprop? As a reminder of what? Well, the paper clip is such an uncomplicated thing, a piece of thin metal ingeniously twisted so it's able to hold a whole host of various papers—scraps, notes, important documents, trivia, significa, et cetera. How can something so apparently fragile keep so many things together?

How can something as fragile as our faith keep our lives together?

Oh, there are Godprops like staplers, rulers, Magic Markers, index cards, too, but quite probably my favorite Godprop—and the one that gives me the most comfort—is *opaquing fluid.* Opaquing fluid is know by various brand names like White Out or Liquid Paper. Opaquing fluid is the magical liquid that covers over your errors, your typos, your unfrotuntae slpi-ups. You brush on the liquid and start all over again—hopefully this time with no unfortunate slipups. Opaquing fluid is forgiveness, an obliteration of a goof with no telltale traces that the goof happened at all. Now, where else will you come across forgiveness like that?

RESIGNATION

Nothing arouses our corridor curiosity more than a resignation. Not a firing. Not even an office affair. The latter two phenomena and/or tragedies usually have a simple explanation. Not necessarily a *nice* explanation or a *justifiable* explanation, but a *simple* one.

Like "Dave was slated to go. He hasn't had a fresh idea in four years." Or "I'm not surprised. Phyllis and Sal were thrown together on the Simpson business. I mean, they worked day and night together. Something had to happen."

A resignation isn't like that. A resignation doesn't evoke a quick and simple explanation. No. A resignation raises a whole mess of questions.

"Didn't she get along with her boss?"

"Does she have another job?"

"Is she leaving for more money?"

"Or responsibility?"

"Or both?"

"Was she asked to resign?"

"Did we try to keep her?"

"Did she tell him off when she quit?"

My own reaction to somebody's resignation varies depending on whether I'm the person being resigned from or if I am one of those corridor buzzers.

When I am the one being resigned from I am forced to show a certain measure of caring, compassion, understanding. But when I am in my corridor role I can be as curious, as catty, as my faulty humanity would have me be.

That's a not so pretty paradox, now, is it? Oh, but we are forced into that paradox constantly, almost weekly if the turnover at our company is fairly high. Yes, the more our corporate doors revolve, the more time we are confronted with the possibility of being genuinely concerned or childishly petty.

So when Susan stops in and lights a cigarette and starts by saying, "You know, John, how much I think of the company and of you personally, but . . ." here it comes . . . I am faced with that awful problem again. I must listen and care and perhaps counsel. And throughout this entire painful (for me) process I must remain true to myself.

How?

Well, it's proved helpful to me when a Susan nervously pronounces her affection (former?) for the firm and me to talk to God while the resignee is stammering the preamble to her resignation. As Susan starts to tell me "why," I ask God "what?"

What is it about this joblife of mine
That people are compelled to tell me

The feelings and motives that prompt their
decisions?
Why is it, Lord, that people come to share
Their deep-seated "whys" and "hows"
With me, a stranger by and large?
Is it guilt? Or a case of nerves? Or what?
Why must we feel forced to explain ourselves
To one another
When You have never asked us to explain
ourselves
To You?

I appreciate the fact that this uneasiness of mine when people bare their souls to me is not such a commendable characteristic. I'm not telling you it's a plus; it's a problem, a devil of a problem for me. But like all my problems—some sillier than others—it's God's problem too. And isn't that ironic? Ironic that I can bare my fears and feelings to Him quite readily and comfortably, and yet I cringe when others express their feelings to me.

As I deal with people like Susan, Almighty Father,
Let me remember how wondrously you have dealt
with me.

And what about the other situation? When you're not the specific receiver of the resignation but rather you run into someone in the corridor who blabs, "Didya hear about Susan? She's leaving!"

That word "leaving"—what a tricky word . . . a dangerous word . . . a word that can lead to assumptions and conclusions that don't reflect well on Susan *or* you.

We should leave "leaving" well enough alone. Try stifling our curiosity, refraining from probing into Susan's career at our place and not reading between the lines of her resignation.

Strange, isn't it, that the problem we might have when someone resigns directly to us is that we *don't* want to know why and what caused it—but when we are not immediately involved in the resignation we *ache to know* the slightest, and perhaps most sordid, details. Complex little creatures of His, aren't we?

NOISE

Jim Plunkett is all wet. He may be able to read defenses well, but he doesn't read business life well at all. When *USA TODAY* asked the Raiders' quarterback what he will miss about football when he retires, Jim answered, "I will miss the crowds. When you have a 9 to 5 job the only noise you hear is that of the air conditioner."

Wrong, Jim, wrong. You can't hear the air conditioner at all. The sounds of business life drown it out. The sounds of 9 to 5 are not hushed like a library's. They're not whispery like a chapel's. No. They are lively and gloriously audible sounds. As audible as *your* audibles, Jim. They are giggles and grunts, yips and drones, rings and buzzes, hums and ho-hos, clacks and thumps, scrapes and scratches, thwacks and coughs, screams and squeaks, groans and hallelujahs. These sounds may not reach the decibel level of a stadium roar after a fifty-yard bomb or a coliseum groan after a critical fumble, but they are just as colorful as those sounds, if not more so.

Drop by my office sometime, Jim, and give a listen. In fact, drop by just before noon when business noise is at its cacophonously beautiful best.

Why is nearing noon the best time for office noise?

Because most of the sounds produced at this time are anticipatory sounds and anticipatory sounds are always beautiful sounds.

And what are the 11:55 sounds anticipating? Lunch, of course. The midday respite. The welcome munchy midday respite. And because we are so avidly anticipating this time of day, you'll hear typewriters clacking more frenetically. Phones ring almost in unison as last-minute plans are made to go out, or orders for food to be brought in are relayed. Desk drawers close with resolute bangs. Shades are drawn, venetian blinds are closed to prevent the afternoon sun from intruding and overheating offices while we folks are out to lunch.

You hear bells ring, signifying fully loaded elevators. You hear laughter and animated recaps of the morning's madness. You hear a phalanx of feet (clogged, sneakered, Florsheimed, espadrilled) hurrying down corridors, going down stairs. You hear revolving doors squeak rhythmically, seeing-eye doors whoosh open and shut. You hear noise, Jim, joyful noise, and unless the air conditioning unit is on the fritz and therefore knocking and grinding away, you'll never hear it at all.

Jane Austen wrote that "everybody has their taste in noises as well as in other matters." We 9 to 5-ers love our noontime noises best of all. Thank God for those noises.

I think I will.

Thank You for all the sounds
That accentuate Your gift of life.
Each one reverberates
Just how wondrous life can be.
Yet I can't help wondering, Loving Lord,
As I revel in this din,
Just how loud are the sounds
In Eternity?

The Cab Ride

American Business, by moving to the suburbs, is said to gain a better working climate and therefore supposedly happier workers. Yet in leaving the city it loses one of its greatest occasions for spirituality—the cab ride.

In the suburbs, 9 to 5-ers can walk to lunch, sometimes only a few hundred feet to the company cafeteria. And if on occasion they must ride to a restaurant, they can do so in their own cars—in relative comfort, on unclogged streets. Pleasant? Sure. But what these cool, unflustered lunchgoers are missing is the opportunity to appreciate God through one of God's most inimitable creations—the cabby.

Is there any profession—yes, even the ministry—whose members exemplify the glory of being as intensely as cab driving does?

A former colleague of mine, born and raised in the mountains of Colorado, was absolutely enthralled by cabdrivers when he moved to New York. In the years that he worked in the city my friend "collected" cabdrivers—that is, he wrote down the name of every driver he was driven by, jotting down also the driver's manners, any noticeable idiosyncrasies, quotes and quirks. Had my friend had the vision to publish his "cabalog" there's no doubt it would have been a sociological marvel of Pulitzer proportions, a tome pored over in psychological salons everywhere.

That's because the cabdriver celebrates being by manifesting three emotions more intensely, I suspect, than any other worker one will ever meet. And those three emotions are Frustration, Passion and Hope.

As for Frustration, no one knows the infernal frustration of traffic the way the cabdriver does. Gridlock (wasn't that the monster in *Beowulf?)* is something the cabdriver must forever dread. Then there's the Frustration of skimpy tips—or the horror of no tip at all. The Frustration of a long and arduous journey summoned fifteen minutes before the cabby is due to go off for the day. The Frustration of waiting hours at the airport for another fare. The Frustration of breakdowns and flats, mean-spirited passengers, heat and overheating, rain and the nagging fear that although he'll put over 150 miles on the meter today, his life is going nowhere.

Many cabdrivers want to talk about their Frustrations, and we who are concerned rather about any Frustrations the client may be about to lay on us at lunch don't really want to lend this cabby even a temporary ear.

Unless.

Unless once again—still, yet, and always—we remember that his Frustrations are very much like ours. After all, where are *we* going? Where are *our* lives headed? What psychological gridlocks do we face every day—situations that render us immobile, totally incapable of making a decision whether to go this way or that?

Can you imagine how something as gentle as a grunt of acquiescence, an "I know . . . I know," or a more expansive "now ain't that the truth!" can help allay some of those cabby Frustrations? Or at least our expressions can give him an indication that someone cares. For a brief time (or forever, if we're caught up together in dreaded gridlock) we can be the cabby's Frustration sponge, soaking up a spate of spoken anxieties of another human being. Wouldn't we from time to time like to have the situation reversed?

Some of us may cringe as we listen to another person's very personal Frustrations, but do you suppose God cringes? Although listening to a litany of a cabby's woes may be unpleasant for us, a cabdriver's Passion, on the other hand, evokes a different reaction. A cabby's Passion usually brings a smile (prayer, not pose) to our face.

Cabdrivers are just about the most passionate people you can find outside of Fenway Park or Wrigley Field. (I know, I know . . . it's *always* difficult to find a cabby outside of Fenway Park.) Cabdrivers can wax passionate on their favorite team, athlete, star, or goat. The language is colorful. The comments, caustic or laudatory, are almost always quotable—and we do, we do. How many times have

I said, "Dave, I gotta tell you what this cabby said to me today . . ."

But a cabdriver's Passion is inflamed by things other than sports, as well. He raves about or raps certain politicians. He screams about taxes. He goes wild about the new Miss Nevada. He paints an unforgettable word picture of his wife's spaghetti sauce. He goes bonkers over ERA proponents. He's passionate about certain TV shows, union leaders, cops, grandchildren, people who smoke. He isn't blasé, that's for sure, and doesn't even care what blasé means.

What's to be learned here? One lesson is this: that although many of us are born and raised as passionate people, we feel obliged to leave our enthusiasms at home when we go to work each day. We get to our place of business and turn on the cool.

We switch to our objective demeanor. We do everything in our power to keep our emotions under control, to be soberly, abjectly *dis*passionate.

But why? Is it because the cool, dispassionate operative is better regarded and rewarded? Do we as a society respect and extol the virtue of androidian aloofness? Why must we feel we can't let out a "yahoo" in the conference room when we've made a sale or a telling point? Is applause to be considered anathema in a corporate corridor? Or can we learn from the cabby who wears his Passion on his sleeveless shirt, who is not ashamed to tell us of his loves and hates, who is not embarrassed by being . . . intensely human?

And along with feeling so comfortable revealing his Passions to us, his fare-strangers, the cabdriver feels just as free to tell us of his fondest, wildest

Hopes. Those Hopes tend to be fantasy Hopes, the kind of Hopes we 9 to 5-ers feel we must stifle while in a (Danger—Cliché Just Ahead) "work mode."

The cabdriver's fantasy wishes are things like a big lottery hit, Bo Derek or Jeremy Irons (depending on the cabby's sex), bowling a 300 game Thursday night, owning his own fleet of cabs, getting her law degree nights (not so unattainable, by the way), a month in Bermuda, a tryout with the Dodgers.

And what about us? What are our 9-to-5 Hopes? Do we have any at all, other than hoping the bus or train won't break down tonight on the way home? Is it too outlandish for us to Hope for things like running the company, getting an on-the-spot firing-line raise, making the cover of *Time?* As long as those Hopes don't fester into obsessions they can be lovely things, phantasmagorical carrots held out there to coax us corporately on.

All this from a cab ride, from a cabby? You bet. Just by examining the intense way he revels in humanity. Then we can confirm once again that he and we were created by the same Being—and most importantly, he and we were created for the very same reason.

Germaine Greer might have been inspired by a cabby when she wrote, "Every time a man unburdens his heart to a stranger he affirms the love that unites humanity."

My Colorado friend had the right idea when he started collecting cabbies. Next time you reach for a tip, tell yourself the tip isn't for the safe, quick ride but rather for the things the cabdriver has just taught you about Frustration, Passion and Hope.

The Business Lunch

This is just about the best time of day for us to be actively aware, even mentally vocal with God. The best time, that is, since the alarm clock buzzed us into reality early this morning. I say "actively" because once we come to terms with the three assumptions expressed back in Paragraph One of this book we will always be "passively" aware of God. We'll always be certain in a sort of harmlessly haughty way that "I'm here . . . He's here . . . so all's well with my business world."

What is it about lunch that allows us to accept God's daytime presence so much more readily then than at other times?

Because it's probably the first time since we slogged out of the shower this morning that we are relaxed—or at least pretending that we are relaxed. That relaxation, real or pretend, may be a result of the restful decor of the restaurant, or our familiarity with the place and its staff, or the vodka and tonic in front of us.

We arrive early. Earlier than our lunch companion. We should always arrive earlier than our lunch date so that we can sit down with our vodka and tonic or Perrier or tomato juice or cheese and crackers and lean back and say, *"God, am I glad the morning is over."*

To which God will reply, *"What do you mean?"*

To which we will answer, as we bounce a wedge of lime back and forth against the walls of the tall glass with our stirrer, *"What do You mean by 'what do you mean'?"*

To which He will respond, *"Are you happy about the way the morning went or are you unhappy?"*

"I wasn't thinking of it, Lord," we will answer, *"in terms of happiness or unhappiness. I was thinking of it just in terms of 'over.' "*

"Over." Volumes could be written about the word and its heavy implications. Well, maybe one volume.

"Over," in this case, could mean we can finally relax from the morning stresses—Susan's resignation and Charley's absence, and all the pettinesses that unexpectedly cropped up.

"Over" might imply that we somehow muddled through the tough part of the day's calendar and the afternoon should be a piece of cake.

"Over" can be looked at pessimistically or optimistically—either that morning is over and we failed, or morning is over and we survived. Now let's go on to bigger and better things in the P.M.

That latter attitude obtains when our pre-lunch companion, God Almighty, tells us *"over isn't such a big deal in My book."*

Hmmmm? Not such a big deal? Why not? We think about it—and it dawns on us that once we acknowledge not only His presence, but also His constant concern for us, then, in fact, our wildest hopes are never over, our ability to do good and be good is never over, and—miracle of miracles—our lives, our very beings will never be over.

Yogi Berra is a nice man and a good manager, no matter what George Steinbrenner now thinks. Yogi's been quoted as saying "it's never over till it's over." Nice quote. Good slogan. Steinbrenner once knew enough to merchandise it, to put it on billboards. But better yet is God's promise that "it's never over—period."

As the warmth of that magnificent premise/promise seeps through our very being (or is that the vodka?) our lunch date, The Client, arrives.

We won't dwell at length on the how-to's of The Client Lunch. So many articles and books have been written on the subject—hopefully, I trust, with tongue firmly imbedded in cheek. "Power lunching" is a popular and hilarious topic. "How to get anybody to do anything you want before the chocolate mousse" probably appears somewhere today in a business school syllabus. Anything I could add to that body of knowledge would probably be confusing rather than amusing. Except my argument that chocolate mousse is grossly overrated.

The point here to be made about The Client Lunch, though, is one that may not have been made, or at least may not have been made emphatically enough, in all that frothy lunch literature. That is, that *The Client Lunch gives us a wonderfully singular oppor-*

tunity to appreciate The Client as a growthsource and not merely as a profit source.

Growthsources are those myriad things around us that help us to mature spiritually, to flirt with perfection if we use those growthsources wisely. Growthsources can be institutions—like universities and homes and organizations and corporations and, yes, even churches. Or they can be the hundreds of people in all walks of life with whom we come in daily contact. Even Clients.

So lunch—although it will have to include an item or two of business for the sake of the Internal Revenue if for no other reason—should be chiefly an opportunity to tap into another hopefully reciprocal growthsource.

And how do we do that?

Like the cabdriver, by not being embarrassed about our lives and loves and passions and by talking about them. And also, asking real and not superficial questions of The Client. And, most importantly, by *confessing*.

Hold it. Don't slam the book shut. Let me explain. Yes, Confession is an inflammatory idea. Confession is a controversial concept. But the type of confession I'm talking about can break down barriers and prompt a sharing of the psyche as nothing else can.

I'm talking about a confession of our humanity.

What are these confessions of humanity? First, let's point out what they are *not*. They are *not* gross ugliness like cruelty or hate. Nor are they admissions of grievous faults that would make Attila the Hun shudder. No, they are confessions of those little things in our lives that reveal us as honest and fallible folks, not the perfectly sophisticated people we so often like to pass ourselves off as being.

These confessions of humanity are meant to show our lunch partners, our VIBAs, that all of us are capable of making mistakes and learning from them. The wonderful thing about this openness is that it encourages openness in return. One revelation prompts another. And as we laugh at each other's humanecdotes we sense where this shared gift of humanity comes from. Where and from Whom.

Some of the confessions I have confessed and have had confessed to me are:

- ordering *ris de veau* expecting it to be a rice and veal dish.
- throwing one's laundry down the incinerator chute.
- numerous automobile blunders, including locking one's paralyzed mother-in-law inside the car with the key in the ignition.
- brushing one's teeth with Prell Shampoo.
- constantly calling someone's second wife by the first wife's name.
- being examined by a neurologist, thinking all the while that you were being examined by a urologist.
- shaving off an eight-year-old mustache by mistake after a very early morning shower.
- losing one's shoes after dancing barefoot in a posh disco.
- drinking the finger bowl.

So what do these confessions say about us—both of us or all of us around the luncheon table? They say what we should often be thinking or even saying to God. Namely:

''Aren't we dopey sometimes?''
''Aren't we funny?''
''Aren't we human?''
''Aren't we alike?''

One more thing about The Business Lunch—*be solicitous of the staff.*

Some of the mildest-mannered business people turn into snarling beasts as soon as they unfold their napkins on their laps. They snap at the young man pouring water, ''No ice—no ice—in Europe they'd never serve ice.'' After the waitress finishes relating the day's specials they say, ''I didn't understand the second one. Could you repeat the specials—and more slowly this time?'' They even ask, in a most righteous bluster, to speak with the owner to ''set him straight on just what pesto sauce is supposed to taste like.''

Why this spite, this posturing? Are we trying to wow our guest by abusing the help? Can't we see that, in our bullying attempt to make an impression, we're more likely to be thought of as an ass rather than as astute?

All it takes to bring ourselves back to our basic goodness is a glimmer of God, a word or two with our Creator, the same words we may have used already a few times today.

As I deal with people today, Father, let me remember how wondrously You have dealt with me.

Lunch With an Old Friend

Every business day does not feature The Business Lunch. But unless you're on one of those "fast and be furious" diets, chances are every one of your business days *will* include A Lunch of some kind or other.

What other kinds of workday lunches are there? Well, one of the most delightful midday breaks is Lunch With An Old Friend. Lunch With An Old Friend offers us the opportunity to exercise one of God's most consistently rewarding gifts—memory.

Over a bowl of pasta or a platter of dim sum you share reminiscences of good times past. Depending on how far back your palship goes you may recall certain mutual schoolmates, hometown folks, former fellow workers. Wrapped up in all these memories, even the ones that tend to be melancholic, both of you bask in the warm glow of belonging. Belonging to a certain time together, to a specific place in a most definite past. Feeling so good about a definite past, no matter how briefly, is especially welcome when your definite present—i.e., a lousy morning—has you momentarily down.

But let's be sure that that "down" *is* momentary. Every once in a while Lunch With An Old Friend can be disastrous. That's when you recall a yesterday so full of promise that whatever the achievements you might have attained in life, they don't seem nearly important enough. You convince yourself that you haven't lived up to your promise, that you have somehow fallen short of your expectations and perhaps the expectations others have had for you. This, of course, leads to instant doubt, to anger directed at some random, unwarranted cause, and to depression. All this at what was supposed to be a swell, memory-jogging lunch.

What a catastrophe! There you are heading back to the office in a deep funk, exacerbated by a mean case of indigestion. Now who needs that?

No one.

But it does happen. One friend of mine told me of meeting with an Old Friend of his for lunch. After the perfunctory greeting this Old Friend said, "Jim, let's get drunk and be somebody." Have you ever heard a more distressing declarative sentence? How's that for a profession of unrealized promise, unfulfilled dreams?

Should such a grim profession surface at our Lunch With An Old Friend, we have the obligation to try to dispel those thoughts even if the dispelling takes us long into the afternoon. It's not enough for us to hope on our own and for ourselves. We are bound to infuse hope in others. We must make our brothers and sisters understand that they *are* somebody even before their favorite scotch trickles past their lips. Arrgh, let's not leave Lunch With An Old Friend on such a forlorn note.

No, these meals are, by and large, beautiful nostalgic affairs, sometimes silly, sometimes even teary. We should (and I'm telling this to myself, too) try to have more of them more often.

Reminiscing should be a tranquil meandering down memory lane. Reminiscing should rekindle good times, not reignite bad ones. James Thurber left us a whole lot of sound advice, this thought among my favorites: "Let us not look back in anger or forward in fear, but around in awareness."

Hmmmm. "Look . . . around in awareness." Intriguing thought—which logically brings us to . . .

LUNCH ALONE

If we don't have Lunch With An Old Friend nearly often enough, we don't have Lunch Alone nearly enough either. Once 11:55 rolls around and we haven't found somebody at the next desk or on the same floor to share a tuna salad with us, we get antsy. We look frantically around for someone to join us "for a bite." Even if it's right there at our desk, we feel somehow rejected if someone's not noshing with us. At least some of us do.

But if the contention proves correct that lunchtime is a most propitious time to allow God into our day, Lunch Alone is absolutely the best way to make time for God. That's especially true if we take Thurber's suggestion at lunch and "look around in awareness."

Slide onto the stool and look around. What do you see? The counterwoman is wiping off the shiny top, setting up your napkin and dishwasher-spotted cutlery and giving you such an expansive smile that you know it's not a pose. The man to the left of you is hunched over his BLT and paperback novel, his body language saying, "leave me alone." The attractive, smartly-dressed young woman in sunglasses to your right picks at her—you might have guessed—cottage cheese and fruit plate. And the thought strikes you that every single counter percher (count 'em—how many are there? . . . sixteen—yep, every stool is occupied—sixteen lunchers) is *quiet.*

Save for the occasional crunch a couple of stools down from a rye toast eater, all sixteen of you are lunching in silence. None of you are talking to one another. None of you are saying a word.

Or are you?

What if all of you—every single one of the sixteen of you, right that minute, there in midlunch—all of you are talking to God?

Stay with that thought for a minute. Looking around in Thurber-awareness can't you imagine that the cottage cheese woman, now squeezing a wedge of lemon into her iced tea, is talking to God about some sort of sexual harassment she suffered this morning? And the man on the other side of you, fumbling for some change to leave as a tip, couldn't he be talking about his daughter's green hair and asking God why?

Sure they could—and maybe are. This may be a unique and historic example of community prayer where the community doesn't realize it's even praying as a community.

And you're one of that happy accidental community. You're alone, but with your fellow lone lunchers you've formed an anonymous *ad hoc* bond with God.

So do try to work in a work day then, when you

lunch alone—alone, but not really alone. Sit with your silent affinity group, all your brothers and sisters of the char-broiled burger, and open yourself up to God.

Whatever words I've spoken thus far today
I hope, Lord, have been spoken considerately;
Now as I sit alone with my lunch and my thoughts,
Do You have any words to say to me?

These few words to God bring to mind an observation by Lily Tomlin who wondered "why it is when we talk to God we're said to be praying, but when God talks to us, we're schizophrenic?"

Walking Back

Unless you're more than a mile away or Hurricane Zoe is blowing up a disaster or you have to be at the Departmental Do-or-Die Meeting in thirty seconds, *walk,* don't ride, back to the office.

A man who was touched by Fordham some years before Fordham touched me inspired his players to "run to daylight." Vince Lombardi's exhortation has—and is still having—its effect. In a no less heroic, although a less body-threatening way, I would like to exhort everyone to "walk to daylight" after lunch.

The halftime of our business day is over. No matter with whom we just spent that halftime (client and God, old friend and God, just me and God), we must now return to the grind.

But why do we say "grind"?

Why should so many of us shuffle back to the office in resignation, and worse yet, in *happy* resignation? Why are so many of us perfectly satisfied to live out our business lives in unhassled anonymity? Why should we merely grin and bear the daily grind?

Why shouldn't we *walk* to the daylight of a better life for us and the people around us, a better life fashioned by specific actions we initiate ourselves during that 9-to-5 life?

Buoyed by a delicious scallopine and inspired by a superb Beaujolais we can, as we walk back to the office, plan how we can do some sublime editing of our communal lives.

A fantasy? Are we a bunch of wacko Don Quixotes? What can we—especially those not sitting in those overstuffed seats of corporate power, hope to be able to accomplish? How can we, whose job descriptions don't include policy-making functions, stand a chance of influencing the world in which we work?

First, by not being concerned about the rung of the corporate ladder upon which we wobble. It doesn't matter. It shouldn't matter.

And second, by daring to believe that, yes, we *can* correct certain of life's uglinesses by our own actions.

Life's uglinesses?

What kind of uglinesses and how?

- Maybe we work in a firm whose products are advertised in one of our country's sleaze magazines, those that demean women and our traditional values. How about starting an in-company campaign to get our company to pull the advertising out of the magazine?

- We work in the Purchasing Department and are constantly being taken to lunch, the theater, the ballgame by a certain supplier. Now a mini-TV set from the supplier is delivered to our office. We grit our teeth, rewrap up the set and send it back with a note, "No more . . . no more."
- We see a worker having the skids greased under his career by the company. Rather than shunning this person we go out of our way to befriend him and learn what's wrong in his joblife or his homelife that we might be able to help correct.
- We're confronted, once again, by that colleague of ours who feels compelled to tell us of his latest sexual escapade while off on a business trip. He speaks of his most recent sexual adventure as proudly as he does of his wife and three kids. Rather than listen in leering interest to this guy one more time we screw up our courage and say to him, "You know, Mike, you're a jerk and let me tell you why . . ."

As we walk back to the office and walk to the daylight of an epically promising afternoon (an afternoon *made* promising by our attitude toward it), let's settle on one glaring ugliness, trivial or monumental, and see how we might be able to rectify it.

The trendy phrasemakers who have given us "power lunching" as a handle should be made aware of this truth: power can be unleashed *by* lunch, *by* the way the mealtime conversation goes and *by* the paradisical way the food is prepared, so that the luncher, strengthened in body and spirit, walks back to the office rippling with his newly realized power and eager to unleash it.

Another Elevator Ride

If we consider emotion to be floors,
Lord,
Might we be able
To go from Fear to Joy
As easily as we go from Four to Sixteen?

What a wonderful thing it would be
(Consider it, please)
To be able to move from Dread to Bliss
With just a few squeaky lurches,
One jostling thump
And, of course,
An unshakable Faith in You.
Amen.

Calling Back

The pile of slips sits there defiantly. The threatening heap says to us, "Who you kiddin'? You're not gonna call these people back . . . oh, maybe one or two . . . but be honest—you don't care about most of those calls, now do you?"

We who have sashayed back to the office rejuvenated by a fine lunch and rededicated to doing wonderful things for humanity are now faced with hard reality. And reality reads like this:

"Please call Betty in Personnel."

"Please call J. W. Herz at Ace Credit Corp."

"Please call your brother-in-law, Henry."

"Please call Mr. Thornton."

"Please call Summit Liquors."

"Please call G. S. Ogleby at 776-9014."

And what's your reaction to all these messages?

"Betty probably wants those evaluation forms that were due last week. If I call back she'll bug me for them . . . it's better not to phone."

''Ace Credit? What are they checking into? Am I overdue to some store? Is Ace a collection agency? No way I'm going to call *them* back!''

''What the heck does Henry want? Why doesn't he call me at home? I'll wait until he *does* call me at home. I don't want to talk to him in the office.''

''Whoops—I forgot. I ordered that case of white zinfandel and it must have come in. Gee, I don't have the money now to pay for it. Dumb to order a whole case in the first place. What a show-off. No, I won't call Summit back and maybe they'll forget about the order.''

''Ogleby? Ogleby? I don't know any Ogleby? Forget him.''

''Get me Mr. Thornton right away.''

How and why does Thornton rate when nobody else does? Well, Thornton is the Vice Chairman, that's how. His stripes get our attention. But why doesn't *everyone* get our attention? Why this cavalier attitude toward people who are either unimportant to us, or whom we consider shunnable for a variety of not very convincing reasons?

As we flip through those telephone message slips, imagine how we would react if one of them read:

''Please call God.''

Would we?

Big Win

Every one of your business days should have one. At least one. Maybe even more. But one for sure.

I'm speaking here of an out-and-out *business* win. Not winning the office Super Bowl pool or picking the Academy Award winners right on the nose (though we'll take a win like that, too) but a victory that is important to the company and your career.

The nature of your Big Win will depend, of course, on the nature of your firm, and your role in it.

Your Big Win may be persuading someone to sign a six- or seven-figure contract, or selling a suggestion on how to increase productivity in the Moline plant, or holding onto a profitable account that was about to leave, or beating out the competition for a new position, title, role, or reward.

And you did it!

And everyone knows it!

Including God.

To whom you take a few moments to say:

Had I set a new record to the 100-yard dash
I would have panted my thanks to You.
Had I wrested away the heavyweight crown
My first words would have been "Thank God!"
But because my win was for something cerebral
Instead of a victory of speed or strength
I too often forget that it's You
Who infused those brain cells
With the capacity to come up with the winning idea.
During these corporate competitions, Almighty Father
May I never ever forget
That You're also responsible for those achievements of mine
That don't require my working up a sweat.

One of the scuzziest notions about success I have ever run across came from the mouth of David Merrick. The Broadway producer said that "it's not enough that I should succeed, others should fail." What kind of perverse joy does David get out of seeing others beaten—or worse yet, of others beating themselves? Does the man really like to rejoice in the failures of others?

When celebrating *our* Big Win we ought to realize that there could well be some people involved in our win situation who are on the losing end. It was *our* idea that was bought; somebody else's idea was rejected. *Our* group was assigned the juicy account over a couple of other competing groups.

We were given the promotion rather than three other candidates.

There is nothing wrong with flashing delight, a display of elation. But the flash should be fleeting, the display a brief one—as brief as the prayer of thanks. In fact, it has been proven a physical impossibility to gloat and pray at the same time.

Dumb Meeting

It's not that the attendees are dumb—although you may have some doubts about Dennis over there, the Chairman's administrative assistant. No, it's not the people, it's the *idea* of the meeting that's dumb.

Stephen Baker, in his book *I Hate Meetings,* writes, "People like to point out that little, if anything, is accomplished at meetings. They are missing the point altogether. The main purpose of having a meeting is to find an excuse for having another one soon thereafter, preferably on the same topic."

And this particular Dumb Meeting will achieve just that, giving rise to many more meetings on the same fuzzy subject. This particular Dumb Meeting is being held at three today in the Board Room to introduce middle management to the newly articulated, but hardly articulate, goals of the firm. And there are the goals, sitting up on the screen in vivid (although unfortunate color choice) red. "OUR COM-

PANY MISSION—PERSONAL PRIDE AND CORPORATE FULFILLMENT."

What does it mean? Well, the Chairman will attempt to elaborate on the subject, the President will try to elucidate, and the Senior Vice President of Administration and Personnel will speak on the implementation of the mission which, it goes without saying, will involve a series of other meetings, proving Mr. Baker's contention.

In some companies, Dumb Meetings dominate the day. In such companies, process is so much more important than product that discussions and explanations of process will be going on in some meeting room or other all day long.

I have seen a number of well-intentioned people—been one myself—struggle to improve Dumb Meetings or to have them abolished altogether. These crusaders have gone so far as to bring alarm clocks into the meetings so that speakers' times would be limited. We have adopted meeting rules like "A decision must be reached before the meeting adjourns" and "Nothing will be repeated in this meeting that has already been written in a report, memo, or other such document," but none of these measures has helped to alter the Dumb level of the meetings to any degree.

We still suffer these meetings. We dread them. Yet, employment being a somewhat more preferable station than unemployment, we keep going to them, even presiding over them every so often.

If Dumb Meetings would, in a manner of speaking, "try the patience of a saint," what is God's reaction to them? I don't know if this subject has even been touched on in our iviest theological schools but—*can God ever be bored?* To search for the answer to that question, why not take God along with you to your next Dumb Meeting?

You may or may not find God capable of boredom. And you just may find another, even more pleasant, way to survive a Dumb Meeting. You see, when you bring along God you have another escape option, another alternative to cope with the tedium. Till now, as we all know, the only way to get through a Dumb Meeting was by . . .

Daydreaming

Why don't managerial gurus and authors of business treatises tell of the delicious benefits of daydreaming on the job? Can't these three-pieced visionaries see how refreshing and productive daydreaming can be? Especially when the daydreams are dreamt during a Dumb Meeting?

The answer is obvious. The swamis of commerce don't want to be accused of being frivolous, flaky, or condoning action unbecoming a nabob-in-the-rough. But these overly sensitive souls don't realize what a mistake they're making, what a thrill they're missing, what a recommendation they could be applauded for.

I can imagine the day when Wharton sponsors a seminar on Daydream Marketing. I can envision the *Harvard Business Review* publishing an erudite piece on "Strategic Thinking and Long-range Planning through Dialogue, Debate, and Daydreaming."

The daydreaming dealt with by Wharton and the *Harvard Review* is daydreaming meant to help the corporation. But there is also the daydreaming that helps us workers personally, first and foremost, solely and selfishly.

We can use daydreaming to our advantage to escape whatever Dumb Meeting we find ourselves in. Since Dumb Meetings rarely require us to respond (at such meetings someone talks at us and doesn't expect us to answer), we can daydream to our heart's content without fear of being found out. Our daydreaming will go unnoticed because, except for the speaker, everyone else will be daydreaming too.

And what are some of the personal rewards, the singular satisfactions that can result from our midafternoon reveries? Lovely things like:

Family recommitment. As our minds wander from the agonizing explanation of Corporate Fulfillment being given by our Corporate Uncle, we think of our life's fulfillment. We might find ourselves doodling a sketch of a house, either the house of our childhood or our present digs. We might mentally meander back to apple trees and kicking piles of fallen leaves and the rich tangy smell of those leaves burning, back when burning leaves wasn't an environmental taboo. And there will always be children around those apple trees, those burning leaves, that particular daydream. Who are the kids? You and your friends? Your children now? Can that fall pastiche be recreated in our life now, today, with the premature sophistication of twelve-year-olds, with the electronic fetishes of our blipping, buzzing lives? Maybe yes, maybe no, but let's give it a shot. We dream. We dream. And we sit there and plan a weekend outing the likes of which we haven't experienced in years. We plan a hike, a ride, a meal, an exercise in family togetherness. Do we know how it will turn out? Is it risky? Sure. But worth the effort.

Gratitude. This daydream begins with a sarcastic thanks as we mutter, "Thank goodness I'm not required to do anything at this Dumb Meeting but sit here and listen," and we logically slip into another thanks. In this daydream of appreciation we're grateful (to no one in particular, no one specific mortal or the specific Supreme) for the extended long-range weather forecast, for the great-looking lawn this season, for the Cubs' seven-game winning streak, for Lucia's giving up smoking, for the contract settlement, for chestnut stuffing, for the drippy nasal passages' drying up, for air conditioning, for the 12.50 percent CD rate, for just enough starch in the blouse.

A new career. "Must I sit here and in rooms like this for the next twenty years, until the kids are grown, until the tuitions are paid, listening patiently to inconsequential drivel and being nicely rewarded for that patience? What else could I do? How else could I earn a living?" And as we daydream the possibilities, the Walter Mitty impossibilities and a surprising number of very real possibilities pop into mind. Open a stationery store? Why not? Travel agency? We've got the energy for it. Take evening courses and get our real estate broker's license? Nothing to it. Or . . . or do we sit back, uncomplaining, watching the profit-sharing pot fill up for a . . . for what kind of a . . . for a vague tomorrow?

A greater appreciation of the opposite sex. Hmmm? Where's this daydream going to lead?

A greater appreciation of God. And here we've come full circle. Some minutes ago we asked if God could be bored the way we can be bored. And are bored this very minute. Then, as a shield against boredom, we took to daydreaming. And now we make God the focus of our daydreaming. Not merely God in relationship to our 9-to-5 life, although if we care to dream about that aspect we should go right ahead and dream. But we may choose to fantasize or hypothesize about any facet of our Godlife. We are helped in this meditation by the white-sound drone of the corporate officer at the rostrum. And over this tranquilizing sound we mention to Our Maker:

This morning I read a line by Flannery O'Connor
Not in context, but just as a line—
Yet that single line, as they say
In polite circles, Lord,
Gave me pause.
Flannery, describing one of her characters,
wrote,
"He had stuffed his own emptiness with good
work like a glutton."
And the thought struck me, Father,
Am I, in some way, like that glutton?
Do I constantly volunteer for do-good drives
Because the causes *are good*
Or because I *will be perceived as good?*
Sure I'd like everyone to think well of me,
But would You rather I do my good work
anonymously?

Call from Home—Stitches

Reveries, by their very wispy nature, are meant to be interrupted. Sometimes they are interrupted gently, sometimes rudely. This interruption is neither. It's polite, but abrupt.

My secretary comes into the Boardroom softly—no clip-clopping clogs, no new-leather squeaks. She comes over to where I'm dreaming and whispers, "Sorry to interrupt, John, but your wife's on the phone and she'd like to speak to you."

I have no thoughts, not even an inkling, that there's any urgency or emergency. Far from it. I'm relieved. I have an excuse now, and a legitimate one at that, to leave this Dumb Meeting.

But that relief quickly vanishes when my wife says, "I'm at the hospital with Josh. He cut his forehead on the locker and had to be stitched up."

What a weird machine the brain is! Well, maybe not *every* brain, but certainly *this* brain. You'd think the first words out of my mouth would be about my son's health, what's the prognosis, how's my wife bearing up. Uh-uh. My response is, "How many?"

And my wife, more puzzled than peeved at this point, asks back, "How many what?"

"How many stitches?"

Now why did I say that? What in the world prompted me to ask about stitches? Was it fear? Was I fearful that Josh had been deeply gashed, that he'd be scarred for life? Or did I speak of stitches because I believe boys have to be tough. After all, they're not sugar and spice. They're puppy-dog-tail-tough. Fourteen stitches is certainly more heroic than five. What a waste five would be! No bragging rights for five, but fourteen—wow! That's worth talking about.

Or did I speak out of stupidity? The stupidity of machismo or the stupidity that comes from simply not knowing what to say? Perhaps I was stunned, just plain stunned, by the emergency and hadn't the foggiest idea how my humanity was supposed to respond.

You and I, of course, should expect emergencies. We should also be prepared to cope with those intrusions in our business lives that whisk us away psychologically, and sometimes physically, to our private lives. No matter how neat and orderly our desk calendar may be, there's no way to schedule our life calendars that perfectly. Emergencies happen and it will be ever thus.

Depending on the news that the interruptive phone call brings, our response may be something from a few comforting (and well-chosen, John, you dummy) words to a hasty flight to your spouse's and child's side.

If until now, until this accident, I haven't realized

that God has been at the office with me, this incident startles me back into some kind of emergency spirituality.

Consider this. As I grab my attaché case to rush off to the hospital, I'm likely to say a few things—in supplication most probably—to God. Aha! Then He's here, isn't He? God is right here with me. And He's been here with me ever since I took off my coat first thing this morning. It's just that—that I never noticed. I never paid attention. It took a slew of stitches to get me to turn to God, to realize that He's been around all day. And now as I dash out of the office I babble to Him:

Come along with me, Lord,
To give comfort, to reassure us
That these cuts and scrapes
Are as easy to mend as . . .
As . . . as my frequent unmindfulness of You.

CALL FROM HOME—FLOOD

If your home is a home for one, the interruptive late afternoon phone call may go something like this:

"Miss H? This is Irwin. Irwin the Super?"

Of course it's Irwin . . . Irwin the Super. Who else could it be? He's the only one who calls you Miss H. You've often wondered why. Maybe four syllables is too much for Irwin to handle—or maybe he finds your Germanic surname too tough to pronounce. At any rate you've grown to like Irwin's way of addressing you and you've grown to like Irwin himself.

What you don't like is Irwin's message.

"Sorry to bother you at work, Miss H. Wouldn't do it—bother you, I mean—if I didn't need your okay . . . which I need if we're gonna move your furniture and take out the rug."

"Move . . . fur—take . . . rug? What are you talking about, Irwin?"

"Seems as if a pipe busted up in the Cassidys' apartment just over yours and, you see, before anybody found it—the Cassidys bein' in Europe and all—a good bit of water seeped through the ceiling and into your living room. Your furniture is wet in some places, but the rug is really soaked—soppin' wet. Oh, we'll get it cleaned and stuff—we're insured for this kind of thing—but . . ."

And what do you do? What's your reaction?

You scream at Irwin. You scream blue murder at Irwin, this Irwin whom you've come to like, this affable pleasant moniker-maker, this diligent superintendent who has done you no ill—you chew him out something fierce.

"Hey, take it easy . . . hey, Miss H . . . it ain't like it's my fault, you know. It's like the pipe just busted—pressure or something. It's nobody's fault . . . it's . . . it's an act of God."

Not really, Irwin. Not even legally, Irwin. A tornado is an act of God in the strict insurance sense. Never heard of a broken pipe attributed to divine caprice.

But the mention of God, in Irwin's flawed logic, does make a dent in your train of thought, and you achingly realize:

When things go wrong, Lord,
Why do I lash out at
Whoever or whatever is nearby,
Blaming them,
Naming them
As the ones responsible for whatever woe
Is laying me low?

Grant me the good sense

And good humor, good God,
When the fuses blow
And the drains get clogged
And the old pipe bursts
To blame those who are really responsible—
Gremlins.

Call from Home—Loneliness

This intrusive call from home isn't a call from *your* home, although it once might have been your home. It's your mother calling. No, she isn't sick, doesn't need money, nothing wrong with the house. No . . . she's just . . . *lonely*.

Here's a twist. The frantic pace of your business day (forgetting the brief respite you just had by daydreaming during the Dumb Meeting) is now interrupted by—loneliness. Not yours, to be sure, but the loneliness of someone important to you.

How you deal with the loneliness of your mother, be that feeling of hers a transitory one or a long-term sadness, is a subject to which you will have to give a good deal of heart-wrenching attention. But as you stand there at your desk speaking on the phone to your mother and you look down the busy corridor, you're struck by the thought that there are a lot of lonely people right here, right now, working with you.

Why, one of the very reasons they *are* working—and often intensely, madly so—is to take their minds and hearts off their loneliness. Like Mario in Accounting who has just suffered back-to-back love-affair failures, the last one called off just a week before the wedding. Like Ann, the terrifically talented research supervisor who is three thousand miles away from her family and keeps telling everybody so. And Ginny, the receptionist who welcomes strangers to the office so warmly and genuinely, but who has inexplicably built an ice fortress around her personal life.

Sure, your mother is lonely and you had better do your darnedest to help her out of her funk, but shouldn't all of us, if we are able and know how, help Mario and Ann and Ginny and their lonely like as well?

There's a rather ludicrous string of descriptives that comes to mind. "Carrier of love and sympathy, messenger of friendship, consoler of the lonely, servant of the scattered family . . ." No, the descriptives aren't ludicrous. They're quite lovely, I think. Wouldn't we all love to have those descriptives applied to ourselves?

What I *do* find silly is that "carrier of love and sympathy, etc." is inscribed in the Washington, D.C., Post Office as a description of that much-maligned—and often justifiably so—agency.

Still, I thank the U.S. Post Office for giving us "servant of the scattered family." It's a wonderful phrase to apply to ourselves. In fact, how about considering it a charge, a directive to work toward that end, to see if we can earn that appellation for ourselves. We should try to earn the right to be called "servant of the scattered family" not only for allaying Mother's loneliness but for easing the loneliness of all our sisters and brothers—those related by blood *and* those related by being.

SURPRISE!

It's a fairly recent phenomenon and a wonderful one at that. In more and more offices you'll see and hear people being greeted in song, toasted and saluted, feted and gifted on their birthday, anniversary, or for reaching some milestone that's worth a little mirth.

These quickie celebrations puncture the business day with a welcome jolt of joy.

BOO ON THOSE COMPANIES THAT BAR THEM.

Louise gets a call to go to Mr. Hobart's office on the seventeenth floor. But Mr. Hobart, when Louise arrives, isn't there. Strange. Puzzled Louise returns to her work station on the fifteenth floor to find—twenty of her co-workers, three bouquets of flowers, a stack of helium balloons and a top-hatted gent with a mechanical monkey playing and singing "Happy Birthday."

And next week it will be Cheryl's birthday and the Tuesday after that Stan in the Duplicating Room will turn fifty and that Friday afternoon there'll be a surprise baby shower for Helene.

Maybe we do care. Maybe during 9 to 5 we *do* reach out to our colleagues and remember them in a disarmingly appropriate fashion.

Maybe we *do* care, but maybe we selectively pick those people who'll receive our showing-of-care. Give it some thought. Don't we limit our surprises to those who we feel want to be surprised?

I mean, it is *Louise's* birthday and we know Louise is an outgoing, fun-loving soul who will find the idea of a cannoli with birthday candles on it (she's Italian) very funny. So we have no qualms about surprising Louise with an expression of joy. She'll love it. We know it. We just know it.

Yet we hesitate to do the same for Mrs. Drummond, the dowdy librarian, and K.L., the senior V.P. of Finance and all those other people who, for whatever reason, seem to us aloof and not the type to take kindly to singing telegrams and balloons with funny inscriptions on them.

Is it Mrs. Drummond and K.L. or is it us? Is it their frosty nature and somber personalities or is it our assumption of what kind of people they are that keeps us from tossing them a twenty-minute bash when the occasion arises?

It could be a little of both. Sure, these *are* reserved people—but who's to say that they wouldn't be tickled with a kicky bit of recognition? And we *are* opinionated people ourselves, jumping to conclusions about who we think is fun and who we think is frumpy.

So?

So let's find out when it will be Mrs. Drummond's birthday and let's do something for her. And let's all pop into K.L.'s office and give him a "It's-great-that-you've-been-here-twenty-five-years" mini-party. Let's try to melt through these people's personal coolness with some horn-tooting tribute.

Oh, there's always the chance that the celebrant really doesn't want to be a celebrant. Dispensing joy can be, at times, a risky business—but then again so can be the acceptance of joy. Both require a special effort on our part—an effort to be human.

And that smile on old K.L.'s face, a real prayer not a rare pose, will make it all worthwhile.

Surprise!

The Expense Report

It's getting late in the business day and you've managed to push it back to the far recesses of your mind. And just not those far recesses of your mind, either. You've also tucked it at the very bottom of the To Be Done pile as well. Ah, but you can't delay it any longer. The Accounting Department is bugging you for it, pestering you for the overdue St. Louis trip expense report.

But since the trip was three weeks ago you've used up much, if not all the $150 advance for personal things. Well, it's pay-up time now, and you better get with it.

So which of these reports will you submit?

St. Louis Trip—October 3

Cab to airport	$ 19.50	
Gratuity at airport	2.00	
Snack at airport	6.75	
Cab in St. Louis from airport to the client office	11.50	
Lunch (J. Skaggs, L. Porter)	74.90	(lost receipt)
Umbrella	15.00	(unexpected rain storm)
Cab to St. Louis airport	11.50	
Drinks on plane	4.00	
Cab home	19.50	
TOTAL	$164.65	
Advance	(150.00)	
Due Employee	$ 14.65	

or

St. Louis Trip—October 3

Drive own car to and from airport, 80 mi. @ .20 allotment	$ 16.00	
Parking and tolls	9.50	
Cab in St. Louis from airport to the client office	8.00	
Lunch (J. Skaggs)	36.50	(receipt attached)

Cab to St. Louis airport		8.50
Drinks on plane		4.00
	TOTAL	$ 82.50
	Advance	(150.00)
	Due Company	$ 67.50

The first report belongs to that genre of literature of which Doctorow's *Ragtime* is a shining example. That is, mixing fact with fiction, with the emphasis on fiction. Yes, it's plausible that you took a cab to the airport, but truth be told, this time you didn't. The same holds true for the snack. Plausible that you should have one. But this time you didn't.

Since no one at your firm has visited this potential St. Louis client, no one knows whether the address is an $11.50 or an $8.00 cab ride from the airport. And who's going to take the trouble to check?

The lost lunch receipt may raise an accountant's eyebrows and the justification for the purchase of an umbrella may be questioned, but look at it this way, the day was a long one and a drag and there really wasn't any business to be done or money to be made with this potential client, so your company shouldn't quarrel with a little fudging here and there, now should it?

The second report is accurate. Oh, the mileage to and from the airport was really 76 miles, but you round it out to 80 to make it easier to tally and the 4-mile difference works out to be only 80 cents more.

So which of these two reports will you submit?

Can't decide?

Talk it over with God.

"It's your *company," The Chairman has told us*
And if that's really so,
Can't we feel free
To compensate ourselves
For our company time
And company trouble
As we see fit?

But You have told us,
"It's your *conscience,"*
And since that is *so,*
Shouldn't we do
What our conscience tells us
Is the right thing to do?

Gray, they say, has become
Our society's dominant color.
But could You, Lord,
Keep my conscience alert
So that I might see
That certain things
Are still meant to be seen
Only in black and white?

THE FIRING

There's an entire shelf of management books that tell us the same thing: *This is the time to do it.* Do it toward the close of the business day when he will have time for private reflection, private anger, without the humiliating prospect of having to face his recent, and now former, colleagues.

"Fire just before five" is the hasty little maxim.

"But prepare for it all day" is my advice to myself.

You just can't ad-lib a firing. You simply can't pull the rug out from a person's career with a matter-of-fact yank and an inappropriate handshake. No, termination takes preparation.

And a big part of that preparation, if not the most crucial part, is prayer. This prayer, unlike most others of the business day, is not a quickie hello to the Almighty. This prayer is slow and thoughtful and tends to be a continuous prayer. That is, you might pray it from the moment you think of the unpleasant task awaiting you until the moment when you carry it out.

More than once during the day you may choose to say:

Good God, Good Guide,
Of my life and his,
May we both come to understand
During this trying ordeal
That our lives are measured
By so much more
Than whatever shortcomings
Interrupt a business life.

Grant that, in the telling
Of why this is being done,
I may make him understand
That we are genuinely concerned
For his well-being.
We, *the corporation,*
And me, *the individual,*
Who all have been
Taught to care
By You, *Our God.*
Amen.

Yet no matter how prepared you may be, strengthened by prayer and armed with notes and points to be made and directions for the conversation to take, sometimes the response from the person whose life you are now confounding takes you aback.

—"John, I'm fifty-two. What am I supposed to do?"

—"John, it's okay, it's okay. I needed this kind of jolt."

—"John, you're going to get yours someday."

These responses are word for word, as best as I can recall them. Yes, they have actually been spoken to me, substantiating once again that we are creations as distinct, as one-of-a-kind, as snowflakes and fingerprints. United as we are by our humanity, we are nonetheless singular creations, each and every one of us, and so our response to various situations—like the trauma of losing one's job—will be singular as well.

What we must be prepared for, then, is whatever we haven't prepared for—that is, an unexpected response from a unique work of God.

That work of God may rail at you or sob, threaten you or thank you. But be prepared for an unexpected reaction. Don't think it silly or stupid, irrational or childish—and for goodness' sake don't tell him you think he's acting foolishly. His emotional display, whatever characteristics it may take, is another manifestation of humanity, the bond you share with him.

He has, in this moment of crisis, chosen to shock you, shake your equilibrium, throw you out of conversational kilter. And what recourse do you have? Do you ask him to leave? Do you leave the room yourself?

Or when someone reacts in pique and heat with a line like, "John, you're going to get yours someday," do you try to arrest his flaring passion with, "Tom, do you ever talk to God?"

Ready to Leave

That question may be asked of you by a number of people with a number of different motives.

"Ready to leave?" says the woman who lives two blocks from you and is a car-pool partner of yours and is anxious to get home to her kids.

"Ready to leave?" asks your secretary, knowing that she has a six o'clock date for drinks and wanting to get home and change first.

"Ready to leave?" says your boss as he sees you slipping something into your attaché case. Is he testing your dedication or just making small talk?

So, "Ready to leave?" is a questionable question whose meaning depends on the speaker and the speaker's relationship with you.

But how about your relationship with yourself? Have you been "ready to leave" since about 10:30 this morning? Has your head "left" the office hours ago, although your body is apparently still here?

Or conversely, do you *not* want to leave? Are you and your head so caught up in the fulfilling frenzy of the day that you want more ego satisfaction? After all, who knows what home will bring? You know you're doing well here at the office. So your answer may be "No, I'm not ready to leave. Let me stay here and luxuriate in my accomplishments for a while longer."

If you think that way you'll be cheered by Proust's conclusion that "work is the only thing. Life may bring disappointments, but work is consolation."

Except, Marcel, taking a chance on life, risking life and reveling in its diversity, knowing full well there can be disappointments, still can bring us joy much richer and more long-lasting than work ever can.

"Ready to leave?" Ready to leave for another dimension of life? Ready to leave for friends or family or fun and games or study or sleep or the movies or the bar or food or love? Ready to leave for another perspective of God?

How's that?

Well, we've been examining our relationship with God in a work environment, in work situations both mundane and critical where communication with God can be meaningful and then some. You can fall back on your Proust perception if you care to. I prefer Van Gogh. The incredibly prolific painter wrote, "I always think that the best way to know God is to love many things." Amen, Vincent, amen.

The Last Elevator Ride

The door opens to a unison groan
From the dozen or more people
Who had hoped for an express,
Only to see one more person
Push into their cage.

Bless all of us, Lord,
As we leave for the day;
And thanks for all your help—
It's good to know that You
Will be riding up the elevator
Tomorrow morning with us, too.
Amen.

Heading Home

One of the greatest gifts lavished on cats, dogs, and us is the ability to doze off almost at will. We humans seem to treasure this gift of snooze most while we are watching TV or heading home from work.

Look around the bus or train or whatever vehicle you ride home in. Just about 74.2 percent of all passengers are napping. Now, if you are riding in a car pool, hope and pray that the 25.8 percent of you that's alert and awake is behind the wheel. But as for you, you're able to let yourself slip gently from one daypart to another. Your chin falls to your chest. The newspaper falls to the floor. And you nap.

Somnologists see these catnaps as beneficial refreshment breaks. Your body and spirit, while in momentary repose, are being rejuvenated. When you awake, perhaps all too soon, your energy, sapped by a tedious business day, will have been restored. You will be ready for family, friends, conviviality, conversation, and meatloaf.

Yes, your body feels much better. That's fine. But have you checked your face?

Although Amy Vanderbilt may not be a source of inspiration for many of us, there is one A.V. aphorism, a syntactically stodgy string of words, that's still quite appropriate for this situation. Amy Vanderbilt wrote that "one face to the world, another at home makes for misery."

What was that "world" face we left the office with? Can you remember? Was it a pleasantly benign face? Or a teeth-clenched, cheek-muscles-taut-and-determined one? Or a drawn, droopy-jawed, the-rotten-day-is-over one?

In our semicomatose commuting state did our "world" face magically metamorphose into some sort of "home" face? Or did we rouse from our headin' home reverie with much the same face we left work with?

Nearly twelve hours ago we looked into our bathroom mirror and examined that face. Some of us, as you may recall, gave some thought to the smile on that face, and even prayed about it. That face, that universal mirror of our humanity, deserves some further consideration here and now as we are about to reintroduce it to people who may be more significant to us than the business colleagues we have just left.

Let's be sure that the first facial message your family receives from you is the one you left home with this morning; namely:

"Happy to be sharing humanity with you,
Here's hoping we're doing right by God
And He continues to deal wondrously with us all."

The expression "here's looking at you" is usually said behind a glass as you raise your drink in tribute to a friend. But what if our literal "looking at you" 's, our faces, sent another tacit message to our friends. What if our "world" face or "home" face, every face said to every other face, "Here's praying at you"?

Which reminds me, I neglected to mention the "transition people" and their relevance to us as we head home. "Transition people" are the people who either help or jar our daily passage from business life to home life. "Transition people" are bus drivers, train conductors, news vendors, panhandlers, traffic cops, and seatmates. They may have an active role in our transition, like the bus driver or conductor, or they may have a cameo appearance in our passage, like the panhandler and seatmate. What is our response to them? Kindness or curtness? Interest or disdain? Do we even notice many of them?

One "transition person" cannot go unnoticed. He intrudes himself into your life in a most blatant way. It's impossible to overlook him. But it is certainly possible to pray for him.

His layered body lops
Out of his vest and onto me.
His NFL thigh presses against mine
And his head,
Attached to a tree-trunk neck,
Falls onto my shoulder.

The dozing stranger next to me
Is more intimate than my children
Who think they're too grown-up
To sleep on Daddy's shoulder anymore.

Should I give the stranger
A gentle jab to rouse him?
No, Almighty Father
Let me instead ask You
To show him (in his sleep)
And me (in my pique)
That if we can live
This close to one another,
Literally and figuratively,
As people,
We should be able
To live much closer
Figuratively and spiritually,
As communities.

HEADING FOR T.J.'S

Between office and home (and sadly, sometimes instead of home) lies an oasis, a psychological decompression chamber, an attitude-readjustment center.

Now, it's not my place nor is it my premise to judge the value of stopping off at a favorite bar for an after-work drink. However, I'd be willing to share my feelings on the subject with anyone who would like to meet me after work for a drink to discuss it. (Oops—did I sort of give away my position?)

At any rate, those who stop occasionally, or regularly, at T.J.'s, The Briars, Maude's or (my favorite name for a bar, especially when you consider it's a block from New York Hospital) The Recovery Room, should realize that by this time they should all feel rather comfortable bringing God along with them. After all, He's put in just as tough a day as they have.

So, as you and your Creator meander over to T.J.'s (meandering isn't all that easy on busy sidewalks during rush hour), give this some thought: *once you get to the bar, don't complain.*

One of our increasingly popular after-work bar rituals, I'm afraid, is complaining about the job and the people we work with. In fact, the practice has become so universal and so refined (although its language certainly isn't) that at least four distinct categories of bar-side complaining have evolved.

In order of increasing intensity the categories are, Whining, Grousing, Carping, and Bitching.

Bartenders are paid and tipped to hear entries in all four categories. But your friends aren't. Including God.

Sure, you may have cause to Whine. Why, you may be justified in Bitching, even. But indignation, righteous or otherwise, just doesn't seem appropriate where and when people are gathered to relax and decelerate. And as the sun sinks behind the yardarm, wherever the nearest yardarm is, shouldn't you and I be more wrapped up in the promise of tomorrow than in the peeves of today?

Words, all those words we have unleashed into our environment since sunrise, have affected scores of people. For their good? For *our* good? Words, you know, are just about the most powerful tools we have at our disposal. With words and words alone we can get someone to put up his fists or put down his weapon. With words we can persuade someone to see a movie with us, change jobs, change allegiances, vote for someone, protest something, buy a raffle ticket, wear plaid pants, join a club, join the Army, join us in bed. Because words are so awesomely powerful, we should be as careful in using them as we are in wielding a breadknife.

At T.J.'s your drink may have a bite to it, but your words shouldn't.

So I suggest that Complaining, all four or more of its identifiable categories, be made as unwelcome at your favorite bar as under-age drinkers. There's a Yugoslav proverb that might look nice in neon hanging just over the cash register. The proverb says, "Complain to one who can help you." And you sense by this time, don't you, Who that really is?

HEADING FOR L.A.

Everyone's business day does not end at five o'clock. Nor at six, seven, or slightly thereafter either. Frequently there are late meetings, business dinners, theater with the client and—arrgh!—a nightcap with the client to contend with.

Nine to five is, of course, a euphemism. A colorful—some say quaint—euphemism, but a euphemism nonetheless. The expression is hardly Rolex-precise. It isn't even Timex-close. But it does mean "business day" and everyone understands that.

Then again as we all know, and have just said, the business day often barges into or blends into the business night. And it often does that on—a business flight.

I really don't care where that 747 is headed—L.A., Houston, or London: I know that the trip, if I'm correctly programmed psychologically, will offer me a superb opportunity to develop my relationship with God.

I said psychologically, but that programming is physical as well. There has to be my customary two V.O.'s on the rocks, and sometimes the ridiculous movie that will never ever make it to neighborhood theaters, and the mystery meat with madeira sauce, and the Fasten Your Seat Belt sign being flashed on during clear air turbulence exactly when the coffee is being poured. It's at this moment that I switch the channel on my headset from the movie to either Dvorak or something by Sondheim—and there's God.

There I am 37,000 feet over Who Knows, Kansas, dreamily ensconced in my nonsmoking aisle seat, finishing off my day on the way to L.A. with God. I defy any saintly hermit to think his cave is any better than this.

I have five and a half hours—on this flight, at least—to lapse into and out of words of gratitude, praise, sharing, storytelling, reminiscing, wondering, understanding my Creator. What a good life He's opened up for me! He's given me so many opportunities, some of which I've botched up, to work wonders for Him and—nothing wrong with saying it—for me too. And for those around me; let's not overlook them. Sure, those around me aren't around me this very minute, but I can think here and now of what these people have done for me through His inconceivable goodness. I remember them and thank God for them, those on earth and those in Eternity. And the thought strikes me that my life and its segments and little boxes and age quadrants—heck, quintiles, almost—have, for the most part, worked out a lot better than I had ever anticipated.

And I remember Heidi. No, not an old girlfriend—and not my daughter's name. Heidi from the story, from the movie that interrupted the Jets game, Johanna Spyri's Heidi, that innocent mountain moppet, *that* Heidi. I remember that she said, "Oh, I wish that God had not given me what I prayed for! It was not so good as I thought."

Well, I've gotten a better deal than Heidi. (There's deal cropping up again.) *It's been better, much better, God, than I thought. Yes, You've dealt wondrously with me and I thank You.*

Sure I'm concerned about tomorrow and the presentation and the nagging possibilities of rejection, rejection of my ideas and perhaps me as well. But there's a resilience, an indomitability that's been built into us by Good Old Master Builder Himself, that will permit us, should we strike out, to come back strong and determined next time up.

So I sit there, white drone of the engines blurring out the chatter going on between Julie the Flight Attendant and a couple of garrulous guys at the cheese tray, and I'm happy with myself because I'm happy with whatever I have going with God.

And I think about the ideas in this book, about sharing my business glitches and disappointments and successes with you, and the ways we might include God in our business day, and I begin to wonder about tomorrow—my tomorrow and yours.

I wonder if after reading the book and giving it some thought we will try too hard, we'll be too intense, too eager to establish a rapport at work with God. Then this voice says to me—my voice, not His voice (although at times we sound an awful lot alike)—"Hey, John, don't rush it. Don't force it.

Don't hurry this relationship. It doesn't have to be tomorrow. Or the day after. There'll be a day when you'll find places to fit Him in. But don't rush it. Take it easy. Let it happen. And it *will* happen . . . in its own God time.''

ABOUT THE AUTHOR

JOHN V. CHERVOKAS, now editor-in-chief of *Madison Avenue Magazine,* was vice chairman of Warwick Advertising and author of that immortal line, ''Please . . . don't squeeze the Charmin!'' He is also the author of *Pinstripe Prayers*.